Best Day Yet

Best Day Yet

Hunting, Fishing, People and Places
Rocky Mountain Memories

Ben O. Williams

WILLOW CREEK PRESS

Published by Willow Creek Press, Inc.
P.O. Box 147, Minocqua, Wisconsin 54548

All photos © Kirby Hoyt, Vintage Doubles and Ben O. Williams

Printed in the United States of America

TABLE OF CONTENTS

DEDICATION

For my three grandchildren:
Andy R. Baker, River R. Lovec, and Kessly K. Lovec

ACKNOWLEDGMENTS

Thanks to John Thames, publisher, and his staff at *Covey Rise* magazine, where these stories were first published, and to the host of friends who penned vignettes for the book. I owe a special thanks to my good friend Tom Petrie, his wife Patti, and sons Ryan and Jeremy, owners of Willow Creek Press, for contributing so many of my "Best Day Yet" times over the years.

FOREWORD

On the way to the SHOT (Shooting Hunting Outdoor Trade) Show in Las Vegas a couple years ago, I made a detour to the Rocky Mountains of Montana for a rendezvous with Ben O. Williams, a columnist for the magazine I was editing at the time. Ben was a hero of mine, and a longtime authority on Western upland bird species and bird dogs—a generational authority is more accurate, as he's raised and trained dogs for more than fifty years, particularly pointing dogs. I knew Ben's byline from my years of editing outdoors magazines, and I was distantly familiar with his fly-fishing chops, too, and his friendship with Joe Brooks of *Outdoor Life* fame. I wrote an introduction for a circa 2000 re-release of Brooks's seminal book—truly a bible—*Salt Water Fly Fishing*, first published in 1950, and knew that Brooks lived his last years in Livingston, Montana, home of the influential Western fly shop Dan Bailey's... and I had heard that Ben Williams worked at Bailey's and helped to organize trout-fishing clubs in that area. It only stood to reason that Ben and Joe Brooks became acquainted. I later learned from Ben that indeed they had. In his study, Ben has an heirloom fly reel that belonged to Joe Brooks.

Shortly after becoming the fulltime editor of *Covey Rise* magazine in 2014, I had talked with Ben on the phone and we played a little bit of the name game from our time in outdoors publishing—my time scant years compared to Ben's decades of writing experience. For many years, he was a regular voice in *Gray's Sporting Journal*, and earlier in my career I worked for the parent company of *Gray's* that also owned a group of fly-fishing magazines I helped run. In that initial phone conversation, I sensed that Ben and I would become fast friends, and we did. I always enjoyed our conversations every couple of weeks when deadlines meant getting a new column from him. I learned that Ben was a schoolteacher for a lot of years, and that made absolute sense to me. My parents were teachers and I worked at a high school for a short while, and I recognized the qualities of the best teachers in Ben. Patience, an ability for expert instruction (of course), diplomacy, empathy, a gentle nature, and virtuosity in the subject matter taught are qualities that Ben possesses. These same qualities also make him one of the best dog men I've ever met. Williams Pride Kennels in Livingston is well-known for its Brittany spaniels, bred and handled by Ben for Western hunting conditions. I say handled because *trained* would be a misnomer—Ben excels at letting each dog develop in its own way and time. He uses repeated exposures to wild birds to draw the instincts out of each dog. This is the way of the best hunting-dog trainers, in my experience.

In my few days as the guest of Ben and his wife Bobbie at their wonderful house in Livingston—which Ben designed, more proof that he's a true renaissance man—I learned those qualities of Ben's extended to fly fishing when we fished the Yellowstone and a spring creek near his home. This was in January, and a mild one, so the weather was hospitable to fishing, though the fish weren't cooperative. No matter. Just spending time with someone as learned and experienced as Ben—and getting to know Bobbie, a little bit—was a lifetime reward for me.

The stories that follow in this book are all vintage Ben; I edited most while working for *Covey Rise*, and each story was a highlight for me during my time with the magazine. Ben's writing is honest, heartfelt, always intends to be instructive, and simply fun to read. I'm proud to call Ben a friend, and I'm excited to read his stories again, this time as an appreciative member of the audience.

Joe Healy

Waterford, Vermont

INTRODUCTION

Right now the magpies and the white-tailed deer are competing for the seed I've put down for the black-capped chickadees, gray-crowned rosy finches, pinion jays, and other songbirds passing through on their way to summer range. The resident sandhill cranes haven't arrived yet, but it won't be long before the pair moves the deer away from the feeding station, as they are quite possessive of their historical territory. That's a "Best Day Yet" on my watch list when they arrive.

Once the winter snows are gone I'll be out on the so-called lawn fly casting, not so much for practice but hoping to get hooked in the tall grass so I can re-create a Best Day Yet in my mind fighting that hundred-pound tarpon I caught years ago or landing that twenty-seven-inch brown trout last spring on the Oxbow.

Sometimes a Best Day Yet is when I'm out with all the dogs in their exercise yard, watching the two young Brittany sisters and the two pointer pups digging the first spring holes, knowing that a half-century ago almost exactly the same thing was happening here.

During the winter I tinker in the studio/shop with my hunting, fishing, and other beloved outdoor paraphilia. But work stops if I let my kennel dogs into the shop and it then becomes an arena—fun-time with tennis balls and doggy biscuits. Having them underfoot brings up memories of each canine's Best Day Yet yearly hunting performances.

Best Day Yet memories, in my view, are meant to last. I don't have mounted game birds or wall fish in my office, or any other place for that matter. My big brook trout's size and shape is locked into my Best Day Yet memory. It's not the fish itself, but the pictures that it calls to mind of a hard mountain walk, hooking a big fish, and seeing a grizzly bear cross the creek as I released the fish. After such a heart pounding, I found a flat rock to sit on and eat a warm tuna sandwich. My greatest trophy was not the fish, but that Best Day Yet event.

Best Day Yet is an attitude that I have created for myself. It's how I feel about things according to my sense of the world around me. It's like sitting by a mountain lake after a wonderful day of fishing with a flask of cheap blended scotch whiskey and believing an airplane dropped a fine single malt scotch whiskey that has just drifted to shore at the exact spot where we are camping.

My partner sitting next to me says, "What do you think of the whiskey?"

"That's one fine scotch... Best Day Yet."

Ben O. Williams

WHAT I REMEMBER ABOUT A BEST DAY YET

–Surrounded by a beautiful landscape

–A meandering trout stream

–Rising trout on a little-known stream

–Releasing a big brown trout under crystal-clear water

–Hunting covey game birds over pointing dogs

–Hunting over multiple pointing dogs

–Dogs on point

–Anticipating the burst of wings

–A flush of wild game birds and a clean shot

–A great retrieve

–A game bird in the hand

–Hunting Huns with vintage double guns

–Hunting with folks that appreciate the habitat as much as I do

–Raising bird dog puppies

–Working with a bunch of young pointing dogs

–Hunting and fishing road trips

–Carrying and cleaning my vintage London Best double shotguns

–Reading a good book

–Having a good single malt scotch after an outdoor outing

–Working in my office with bird dogs at my feet

–Taking but a few birds for the edification of my dogs and the
  glory of the table

THE SOUTHERN WAY
Bobwhites make for a memorable hunt.

Game birds live in wonderful country, places I wouldn't see otherwise. Bird hunting memories span all of my life. I can place them from the 1940s to the present and each one is connected to a place in time. And with time the memories become more valued and joyous.

The places I have hunted are forever marked in memory by the landscape and a human antiquity of long forgotten folks who I nonetheless feel I have known. The feelings grow strongest when I return to a place another time and see my memory landmarks erased by human progress. Some of my favorite bobwhite covers have touched me in this way.

Bobwhite quail once had a wider distribution than the other five species of quail indigenous to North America. And at one time bobwhites were found throughout the Eastern, Southern, and Midwestern United States. This area covered about half of the United States, giving bobwhite hunters a variety of ways to pursue their quarry.

There are more ways to hunt bobwhites than the kind of dogs that hunt them. There are more philosophies of how best to use dogs to hunt bobwhites than ways to transport them. And there are also more opinions of the kind of gun one should use on bobwhites than for any other game bird.

But in the South, that is the Deep South, quail hunting has a long history and is quite different compared to other regions of the country. This form of bobwhite hunting is steeped in tradition and rivals that of college football. It's as traditional as cornbread, hush puppies, and grits.

To the Southern gentry, bobwhite quail hunting is mule-drawn wagons, dog handlers on saddled horses, double guns (side-by-sides), pointers, a Labrador retriever next to the wagon driver, and a plantation's hunting course to follow. To these folks, wild bobwhite quail are the best of all birds for dog work. Pointers are so consistently a part of bobwhite hunting that it's hard to imagine hunting without them.

With the growing popularity of owning a sporting dog and of the relatively new recreational sport of sporting clays, the growth of upland game bird hunting in North America has been phenomenal. This is also true in the South. And when there is growth, you have change.

For good reasons, some Southern plantation hunting traditions have changed, but certainly not their Southern hospitality. Today you can ride a horse, a utility vehicle, or a quiet, sneaky golf cart. Besides the slick, long-tailed pointers other pointing breeds have crept into the Southern plantation scene along with the nontraditional methods of transportation.

I've been fortunate enough to hunt the true plantation way and most of the newer ways. But no matter what type of Southern quail hunting you do, there is a feeling that you are a part of a great American tradition.

Anyone who has carried a shotgun while walking the prairie or riding a mule-drawn wagon through a plantation remembers for a long while the special times and places some of which they may never see or feel again. For me, it has been more than 15 years since I last saw those two lovable burly big-eared mules walking the described course. I can still remember that first rock-solid point. And after walking past the two dogs there was an explosion of wings in all directions. Gun ready, the birds buzz off over the brush and through the pines. Afterwards the two dogs stood there with the superior looks only a successful Southern pointing dog could achieve and continued to point. But let's not forget in other regions of the country this whole deal would take on a different look and a different playbook.

My everyday hunting vehicle consists of a pair of strong legs, lug-soled moccasin type boots, well-worn hunting pants, an orange vest, and a baseball cap. This suits me fine, no matter what kind of bird hunting I do. But having mentioned my preference for mobility, I still have to admit that riding a mule-drawn wagon is rewarding and I'm delighted to have had the chance to hunt in the grand Old South style. Like me, maybe you might like to collect some memories beyond your living radius; it's still out there for anyone to do.

PHEASANTS?
Steve Smith, Editor, The Pointing Dog Journal

Ben Williams' home is the best bird-hunting lodge in North America. Trust me, because in the twenty-five years I've known him and been his editor, I've been there sixteen times.

There are some constants at Ben's place when you go bird hunting. First, you don't rush—let the birds, the Huns and sharptails, feed and head for loafing cover, so, say ten o'clock is about right. You load up six or eight dogs and drive a short distance to a piece of the thousands of acres where Ben has hunting rights. You turn loose maybe four dogs and follow them, staying on high ground if you can.

The dogs, his Brittanys and pointers, point, back, and retrieve. The coveys of Huns and flocks of sharptails are plentiful, and Ben practically has them named. You shoot a Ben Limit, which is half the state limit, and about that time, the sun is starting to sink and it's cocktail hour. That time may come back at his house, or it may come while you're driving down a ranch road. Five o'clock? The truck slides to a halt, Ben drops the tailgate, and pulls out the good scotch and a couple lawn chairs. Then you head for his home and one of Bobbie's great gourmet meals.

I know of no one more dedicated to these two great bird species than Ben, but he's that way with quail, too. Pheasants? Not so much. Once in Kansas, Ben's dogs pointed what we thought was a covey of bobwhites, but when I walked in and flushed, two rooster pheasants cackled skyward. I dropped them both, turning to Ben with a big grin on my face, only to be greeted by, "I hope you're done making all that racket—you're spooking the quail."

I have been lucky enough to know some of this country's finest and most famous wingshooters and dog men, and I can tell you for a fact that there is only one Ben O. Williams. You can look all you want, but you won't even find any pieces of the broken mold.

THE PRAIRIE WAY

A classy bird, wherever you hunt.

There is a notion across North America that good bobwhite quail hunting is gone for the average bird hunter. I disagree.

For the past 25 years, I have focused my bobwhite quail hunting on the prairie states. Iowa, Missouri, Nebraska, Kansas, Texas and Oklahoma all have the potential for high-quality population numbers, so it's just a matter of gathering updated information to decide how, when and where best to hunt.

Midwest bobwhite hunting can be done with a professional guide, working out of a lodge, or on lands open to the public. Being a traveler with numerous bird dogs, I prefer public access programs or state and federal public lands to hunt.

The latitudinal range of the bobwhite is immense. Hunting quail in the Midwest northern tier is different than in the southern reaches of the United States. In addition to the climate differences, the habitat and landscape changes within the bobwhites' world revise the hunting dynamic. Thus, whatever latitude one chooses to hunt, success depends on keen ecological observation of the birds' habits and habitat within that environment.

The way of most Midwestern bobwhite hunters is the "boots on ground" approach, walking hard behind pointing dogs, shooting wild birds using an automatic or pump shotgun, hunting the singles after the flush and driving in a pickup, bone tired.

As in the South, Midwest quail hunting is also a tradition, but the ground game differs in style from place to place. Take, for example, a Kansas hunt I made a few years ago.

That day, it was relaxed with little snow on the ground. After traveling several miles down a wet gumbo road, I encountered a walk-in sign surrounded by superb bobwhite cover that caught my attention.

There was no evidence of any other hunters, so I parked near an old stack of quarried sandstone fence posts. Because of the lack of trees, farmers drilled, chiseled and split sandstone into 12-inch square fence posts 8 feet long to surround their property, a hearty heritage and a task of Kansas pride.

As I stepped out of the pickup truck, a slight breeze welcomed me. A windbreak of Osage orange and black locust lined the picturesque homestead, a story told of folks long forgotten. The crop fields were small, having many edges and intersected by woody covered fencerows. Still other parts of the prairie homestead were much like they were before the settlers arrived.

Clumps of chokecherry with little understory dotted the long fence line, and the sandstone posts looked like sentinels guarding the homestead boundaries. A covey of quail watched my arrival from its safety under a canopy of cover and then scurried out of sight.

On one side of the fence, small patches of snow still dotted the sea of little bluestem that seemed to reach outward toward the pale blue horizon. The field was full of tall milkweed, their empty seedpods turned skyward. Below the milkweed, the rust-colored little bluestem swayed back and forth. On the other side of the fence were rows of shucked corn stalks strengthened by good summer rains. At the far end of the field the land pitched downward, forming a large slough circled by shining sumac, its dried red fruit glistening in the sun. Across the shallow slough were a hardwood forest and then another cornfield.

"Picture perfect for quail," I thought.

I put two dogs down–Hershey, a Brittany, and Misty, a pointer. They hit the ground running. After several relocation points along the fence, a single quail flushed fifty yards ahead and flew toward the end of the field.

The dogs worked both sides of the fence and made several more casts in the open fields, but with no success. So I headed in the direction the single bird flushed, hoping to learn the scattered covey's whereabouts. Once the dogs swept the grassy slough, they slowed to a crawl upon entering a sumac patch. It was not long before they connected. I was pleased the dogs had found the covey.

With two birds in the bag, I turned my attention to hunger. I started up the easy grade walking back toward the pickup. A slight breeze moved the open seedpods. Both Hershey and Misty ran hard out in front of me. With their heads high, they locked up like two white prairie fieldstones.

After the flush and the blur of wings, the 28-gauge side-by-side shotgun sounded a crisp shot that echoed across the slough and into the trees. Several feathers drifted down windward, settling on the mixed grass prairie.

"No need to hurry," I said. "We have all afternoon to hunt."

HABITAT
Brian Carroll, DVM

I am watching my grandchildren play with the pup I picked out for Ben. The whole litter, ears flopping, tails wagging, chasing giggling kids. At this stage of life, there is little that brings more joy than that. Before the grandkids came along, just watching one of those pups make its first find would suffice. As a young man, walking past the point and emptying my A5 was required.

I have kept a kennel of pointing dogs (mainly pointers) since I ventured off to college. I have had as few as two and as many as eight through the years, but they all became part of the family. I raise a litter of pups every six or seven years to replace the veterans lost to natural attrition.

The dogs and I have learned together the habits of bobwhite quail during the November to January season in the mixed-grass prairie of western Oklahoma. They whistle off the roost at dawn, usually in an open area on a little higher ground. Then they mosey down to the breakfast buffet in the ragweed bottoms to feed. After feeding they make their way to overhead cover in fence rows, shelter belts, sand plum thickets, scrub oaks, etc. to dust and gravel while protected from the Cooper hawks during the middle of the day. They reverse the process back to the roosting area later in the afternoon, often close to where they started the day.

It is the human's job to identify country with suitable habitat and the canine's task to cover the country searching the most likely spots for the time of day and conditions to locate birds. It is very exciting and gratifying to watch the "light come on" in a young dog as it learns by repeated exposure to use its instincts and keen senses to race to the most likely objectives, make scent, and point birds.

Ben's photography and prose in various periodicals through the years put a craving in me to hunt sharptails and Huns on the vast prairie of his native Montana. I made my first excursion in 1997 and will (God willing) make my twenty-first yearly trip this fall. I knew nothing about the habits and habitat of these species and had a pretty steep learning curve in spotting the right landscape in which to let the dogs out. I learned to read between the lines of *Wingshooter's Guide to Montana*, and later on *Western Wings*, and in due course could recognize coveted ground while driving down the highway, just as I can in western Oklahoma.

My canine colleagues also had to adapt, first to simply open up and run big to match the immensity of the country, quartering big and wide, and then sifting the wind above the sea of grass to recognize worthy objectives in the landscape. The elevation changes much more drastically out here, a significant fact to keep in mind. Subtle changes in the vegetation are important: green forbs in the low spots on which to feed, soft grass on the slopes in late morning great for sunning, Snowberry patches are the western equivalent of my home plum thickets. And don't stop before the rocky outcropping at the head of the coulee, for it often holds Huns. To watch the dogs make this discovery repeatedly as they make the transformation from Mr. Bob in the tall grass plains to high prairie birds makes the 1,500-mile trip seem like a morning jaunt from Edmond out to Ellis County.

It is almost as much fun as watching the grandkids play with those dogs as puppies...

THE VALLEY QUAIL WAY
Head to the Northwest for an enjoyable hunt.

Over my shoulder, I'm carrying a Browning over-and-under 20-gauge shotgun, walking a typical Western sagebrush draw with a dry creek bottom meandering through it. As I hunt alone with two dogs, it is not long before a trickle of water gets my attention. Because valley quail like woody cover, it just makes sense to investigate the water source.

A well-worn cattle trail with patches of cheatgrass strung along each side is an open invitation that leads to a spongy seep. A tangle of buffalo berry bushes, scrub chokecherry brush and other hardwoods squeeze the narrow draw. Wild blackberry vines climb, fingerlike, along deep crevices up the hillside. I stop to listen for valley quail calling.

"Oh-HI-oh, oh-HI-oh, oh-HI-oh."

Well ahead, the two dogs approach the first stand of buffalo berries as a bunch of quail flush in a roar from across the draw, landing in the sagebrush hillside. More flush and settle in a long string of blackberry briars. Other birds run under a canopy of cover toward the chokecherries. I hurry my pace. The running quail flush in a wave, scattering among the group that landed in the sage. Five or six more birds come out from the other side of the draw and join the main group.

We cross the deep draw and start up the slope. The birds are calling everywhere. On the way up, I pause to watch a quail running through the sage ahead of me. Both Gina and Lola point momentarily as a little dark blur screams by. Without thinking, I swing and snap off a shot. The quail plunges into a sage bush and feathers follow, drifting above the sage tops. Gina picks up the small cock and drops it at my feet. I smooth the bird's iridescent topknot and slip it in my vest.

Within seconds, Gina slams to a point ahead of me and, like a swarm of bumblebees, more quail flush. I miss twice, then almost step on a bird as it buzzes away before I have a chance to reload. Moments later, Lola points a bird that is under her nose and I center it with a single shot. Then both dogs point in front of me as three birds flush, skimming over the sage tops. Just as I get on one of them, it drops in the sage and I shoot too high.

With the dogs at my feet, I sit against a large rock and write down the number of birds scattered above me. A cool and moist breeze fans the sage. After a fine lunch, with quail music surrounding me, we return to the canyon slope to hunt again. By late afternoon, the whispering sagebrush delivers a wonderful hunt that is flagged in my hunting journal.

Today the valley quail is the most common and widespread quail in the West. It is found in the interior agricultural valleys, desert edges and the lower elevations of Washington, Oregon, California, Idaho, Nevada and Utah. Valley quail inhabit hardwood thickets full of overgrown cover, unmanaged hedgerows, abandoned homesteads and shrub brush prairie, all of which have dense cover for escape routes.

I can trace my valley quail hunting as far back as the 1960s. Since then, I have learned a lot about them.

Valley quail are quite vocal and can be heard a long way off, so listening is an important tool in locating birds. Once found, valley quail have a habit of flying only a short distance and are easily found again. It is best to give the birds a little time to lay scent down before pursuing them. Most experienced bird dogs learn how to handle a bunch of running valley quail. So it is just a matter of a dog working the scent until the covey either fans out or flushes. Once scattered, many will run only a short distance. Some will hide individually; others will form small groups and hide together.

It's also important, once a bird is found, to cover the rest of the ground thoroughly, starting with a small circle and enlarging it as you go. When broken up, valley quail hold extremely tight, so covering the same ground over again usually brings results. The fact is, once a covey of valley quail is scattered, it holds as tight as bobwhites.

Of all the game birds native to the Western states, none is more enjoyable to hunt than the valley quail. I'm willing to bet that hunting a bunch of scattered valley quail over a pointing dog will get your undivided attention, quicken your instincts and sharpen your senses.

WESTERN UPLAND BIRDS
Robert Siler

Spending most of my early hunting years chasing bobwhites in North Carolina, I found that their lives were fairly routine, whether in agricultural or forest lands. It seemed that populations were stable from year to year, but in the late 1980s they started disappearing and by the mid-1990s they were mostly gone.

My hunting buddy, now-retired North Carolina quail biologist Terry Sharpe, and I ordered books, called in a few favors, and wrote Ben O letters, while planning for hunting Western birds. We read Ben's books and visited Ben several times. We had numerous and very humorous phone conversations where we asked a lot of questions. What amazed us was that if you asked someone west of the big river a question about upland birds, you got very helpful information; however, if you asked the same questions, east of the big river, you would get: "What? There ain't no birds here."

With Ben's help, we have hunted Montana, Idaho, Oregon, Nebraska, Kansas, Arizona, New Mexico and Oklahoma since 2004. As biologists, we study the birds and the habitat that we hunt. While numerous species of upland birds occur in the West, their abundance is often influenced by similar factors. We found that the lives of Western upland birds are much more complex that their Eastern relatives. Generally, rainfall is the Western birds' lifeblood, but it can be a blessing or curse; timing and severity is everything. For example, good localized rain in an area of Montana during 2010 resulted in a tremendous crop of crickets and grasshoppers and a concomitant surge in sharptails and gray partridge, unfortunately never to be seen on that ranch again. Conversely, in 2016, abundant localized rain eliminated upland birds from an otherwise upland bird–friendly ranch, likely by flooding nests or killing young chicks.

We are always surprised when we hunt New Mexico and find how scaled quail abundance can vary by year and location, largely determined by the quantity and timing of rain. Late rain seems to result in abundant grasses while earlier rain seems to benefit forbs. Similarly, food items of upland birds vary by locations and years, whether it be in Kansas, Montana or New Mexico.

Western prairie lands can be massive and diverse. Grazing and crop production are often interspersed with natural prairie. Upland birds can, and often are, opportunistic, utilizing feed lots and grain fields and avoiding heavily grazed areas. Over the years, we have spent a good amount of time on "dry" hunts, some out of curiosity and some out of stupidity, and have driven many of mile searching for the best habitat to hunt.

I often ask Ben how the harsh winter will affect bird populations; his reply is, "Our native birds and even the gray partridge can survive the winters, as for the Chinese bird, who cares?"

After a number of consecutive years hunting Western states, we are no longer surprised when we hunt an area that was excellent the year before, but now contains few upland birds. We don't pretend to be experts but enjoy hunting pretty areas and attempting to figure out why the birds are present or absent. With the help of local experts like Ben O, we have had some success with the Western birds, and enjoyed exploring many a mile of the Western prairies and deserts.

BIRDS ON THE RUN
Look to the ground, not the sky, when tracking scaled quail.

There is an arroyo with an underground stream that supplies water to a large desert grassland plain. Scattered rows of sycamores mark underground water. This is a haunt of scaled quail, but it once was occupied by outlaws. The outlaws are now only recorded in history, but the scaled quail remain in good numbers.

Not long ago, dodging thorny shrubs and clumps of cactus, I drove over the winding desert trail that led to the bandits' abode. Other than me, only a few cowboys used the sandy trail.

I'm never surprised when I see a bevy of scaled quail on the abandoned road. At first, the birds are almost invisible, as they match the surroundings. They do not attempt to fly; instead, they scurry down the sandy lane with remarkable speed, their heads high and cotton-tops erect. They zigzag through the grassy desert cover. Soon they are out of sight but reappear, crossing a sandy opening far ahead.

I park under the large sycamore not far from the bandits' hideout. My two Brittanys, Shoe and Daisy, race for the water tank straight out of the hunting rig. I walk toward the windmill. Its twirling shadow highlights numerous quail tracks on the ground. The dogs jump out of the tank, their bellies dripping, and shake water ten feet in all directions on the dry sand.

Then suddenly several white-crested, bluish-gray birds dash away in a blur of running feet. At least forty quail flush and fly over a low, grassy hill. Both Brittanys begin to work vigorously and abruptly point. Still other birds run up the hill in the direction of the flushed birds. Daisy breaks point and dashes through the running birds, flushing them over the hill.

I carefully work diagonally across the hill to the top of the ridge and look into a shallow basin of golden grass and low shrubs. A sandy, mesquite-lined wash runs through the basin. As I walk the ridge on this cloudless, warm day, the wind feels stronger. Looking back, I see the windmill still moving slowly. I stop to let the light breeze cool my face.

The dogs come alongside and I stand between them, looking into the desert grassland basin. By the time I load the Browning 20-gauge super-imposed shotgun, the dogs are pointing in the presence of quail. I'm thinking, "How many times have I lived this moment?"

The scaled quail is known also as blue quail, scalie or cotton-top. Their range overlaps that of the other desert quail, but not the same grounds. The country it frequents is barren and dry, associated with scrublands and desert grasslands where the air is thin and the wind is a descendant of the grasses.

Scaled quail are native to the arid desert grasslands of New Mexico, Arizona, Colorado, Kansas, Oklahoma, Texas and Mexico. I got my first view of scaled quail in the panhandle of Oklahoma when they crossed a dirt lane a mile after I turned off the blacktop. Since then they have held my interest.

We frequently are reminded that the scaled quail's sporting qualities are inferior compared to other quail because of the bird's bevy instinct and its ability to continuously run in open grassland country. We also hear that pointing dogs are of little use.

There is no secret formula for successfully hunting scaled quail, only experience. You learn by watching, listening, observing the bird's habits and recognizing its habitat.

Here's my advice: Choose suitable country with stands of good, grassy cover that stops and holds the birds from continuously running. I use big-running, seasoned pointing dogs to find scaled quail.

When the birds are found, the dogs push them until they flush, because they are not going to hold anyway. Once fear grips the bevy from being pushed hard, the quail will scatter. A scaled quail is a strong flyer and goes farther than other quail because of the open country, so keep a careful eye on the direction of flight.

Go after them with intensity where the bevy puts down. Be persistent, covering the ground thoroughly. When a bird or two is found, the rest will be nearby. Once the bevy instinct is lost, the birds hold tight but will call to reassemble.

With most game birds, I hunt with precision. With scaled quail, however, I hunt more with notion.

NEW MEXICO CONNECTION
Ben Brown

Ben and Bobbie came into our lives a little over twenty years ago, along with two little Brittany females, one of which, Freckles, became my best-ever bird dog. My wife, Crystal, and I had the good fortune to spend a month or so each year for about ten years with Ben and Bobbie, prowling the ranch that I managed and hunting with an incredible array of sportsmen and women. We also shared many interesting and fascinating dinners—sometimes with guest hunters in what we called the Long House and other evenings just the four of us at our house. We met and got to know not only luminaries from the world of bird hunting, but also poets, authors, editors, publishers and a sprinkling of business men—all of whom were avid bird hunters. They came to hunt with Ben, the "guru" of western bird hunting.

But it wasn't all about hunting and bird dogs. I remember Bobbie and Crystal going for long morning walks accompanied by Lulu, one of our barn cats who apparently decided that they would benefit from feline company. And as the sun went down, Bobbie and Crystal would often share vodka martinis at our kitchen table. We explored archeological sites where the Casas Grandes people constructed and lived in large pueblos, some with ball courts, seven to eight hundred years ago.

We also visited Ben and Bobbie at their place outside of Livingston, Montana. Ben persuaded Crystal, raised a desert rat, to wade into the wide Yellowstone out back and learn to cast a fly rod. And he introduced me to the Hungarian partridge, a bird that I had not hunted on my previous visits to Big Sky Country. Before I met Ben, I had bred, raised and trained my share of pointing dogs and retrievers, yet Ben taught me more than I ever thought there was to know about bird dogs and bird hunting. I will be forever grateful to Ben for sharing his knowledge, but most of all for his friendship.

GAMBEL'S QUAIL
*In the hardscrabble Southwest, these quail are
considered the jewels of the desert.*

I've always been reluctant to take a partner along when I hunt the singing windmill arroyo, whose loveliness and loneliness seem to demand solitude. Still, sometimes I relent and feel I have to share it.

In desert country during quail season, the sun is warm and the air is moist and smells sweet and tart. The cheerful call of the Gambel's quail—*con-chi-ta, con-chi-ta, con-chi-ta*—is a characteristic sound reminiscent of many soundtracks in western b-movies. This native bird's popularity in desert country is equal to the bobwhite's in the Midwest and the Southeast. Sportsmen travel hundreds of miles specifically to hunt the Gambel's quail, and thousands of acres of public land in the Southwest make this resource available to all.

The Gambel's lives in harsh but beautiful country, made up of gulches, draws and sand washes that lead away from the major arroyos into the hills and ridges dressed in mesquite, cactus, yucca and rabbit brush. Hunting these desert jewels successfully involves learning the birds' characteristics and how their behavior relates to the physical features of the land.

The Gambel's quail is a fast, small target and can give any upland bird hunter pure shooting thrills. And while the birds present some of the best wingshooting the Southwest has to offer, you may also find yourself gripped by a passion for the breathtaking arid desert. In morning, the low light seems like magic, casting long shadows across the cacti-studded landscape. In the high midday sun, the desert is wrapped in its own beauty. Evening takes on a different light, one that softens the harshness of the sun and land and transforms the desert into a world of stillness.

On one recent hunt, the temperature was in the sixties with a moist breeze blowing; it was warm for this time of year. In the distance, cumulus clouds hovered over the range of mountains, but we were headed in the opposite direction. Once out of the truck, the dogs pushed windward and disappeared out of view down the sandy two-rut lane toward the abandoned Ethel Kelly Homestead. I took out a Westley Richards sweet little 28-gauge side-by-side, threw the gun up to my cheek, looked down the barrels, and rubbed the highly figured walnut stock while Ben, my hunting partner, uncased his double gun.

The desert cover gave off a soft amber glow, though the rabbit brush still held its muted, pale-green colors. We walked in the direction the dogs had gone, following the sandy road toward the singing windmill. The dogs found the water before Ben and I got there, their bellies dripping as they forded across the wide and meandering arroyo.

Tracks were everywhere and it was obvious a large covey of quail had moved into the tall rabbit brush ahead of the dogs, whose beeper collars changed to the pointing mode each time they stopped.

"Gambel's on the ground," I said and motioned to Ben.

Experience has taught me that two important maneuvers need to be executed at this moment: First, when a large covey of birds is found it has to be pursued quickly; second, a hunter cannot keep up with a running covey of Gambel's quail, so it's up to the dogs to push the birds into flushing. As a general rule, when a large flock of desert quail is found, the birds must be scattered before there can be close shooting.

A single Gambel's quail flushed out of the rabbit brush to my right. Without shooting, I marked the bird down on the grassy hillside above us. After several more staunch points, the dogs finally caught up to the large bunch of scampering Gambel's. With a tremendous roar of wings, they flew in the same direction that the single bird had flushed.

The dogs also knew the birds' approximate location. By the time Ben and I walked up the hill, they were locked up like stone sculptures. Ben walked in on the first point as a single quail got up and peeled off down the hill. At the shot, the bird tumbled and feathers drifted, following a current of air that hugged the contour of the hill.

After collecting several more birds from their escape hideouts, we returned to the sandy quail highway and scattered a fresh covey. Now with tired dogs and empty hulls, the decision to quit made sense.

We loaded up the dogs, lightened our vests, and took a moment to smooth the beautiful birds' feathers and lay them down in a row, their topknots casting long shadows on the golden sand.

GENTLEMEN HUNT HUNS
Roger Catchpole

Let's be honest, Huns aren't straightforward birds to hunt. And most hunters won't expend the boot rubber required to locate a single covey, let alone to bag a limit. Take it from me, those seeking a leisurely hunt best look elsewhere.

For those who stay the course, Huns will deliver a hunting satisfaction that is unsurpassed. This fascinating covey bird is elusive in flight and unpretentious in appearance. Both traits add to the challenge in harvesting a bird. Still, these factors provide handy excuses when you miss, which all Hun buffs do.

While wingshooting attracts those of all persuasions, Hun hunting seems the preserve of honorable men. Not necessarily men of means. Simply those who are prepared to persist without guarantee of success. People for whom spending time in the field is less about pulling the trigger and more about working their dogs. A more appropriate term for this divergent band of hunters is, perhaps, gentlemen.

You can hunt Huns with most any shotgun. Certainly, they all scatter shot sufficiently well to take a Hun when swung precisely. Yet, the Hun hunter is particular about what he carries. Whether it's a best sidelock side-by-side or a basic over-under box lock, the Hun hunter prizes his gun.

Admittedly, some shotguns are more handsome than others. But the Hun hunter knows that the fit of his shotgun is key. Without a well-fitted shotgun, and quarry familiarity, cutting a feather is but a distant dream. So, beware the man with one gun.

When I first visited Ben O. Williams I took an over-under shotgun. He looked it over and commented on what a lovely gun it was. He was being polite of course; we both knew the truth. But that was my one gun. Today, Ben favors fine English sidelocks and the older the better. Although, I happen to know that he has shot more Huns with a Belgian-made Browning superposed than with any other gun he ever owned.

So when fate intervenes and you find yourself in the field chasing this worthy game bird, just remember to smell the grass, praise your dogs, appreciate your gun and respect the birds. For the reward of a hard day on Huns is not measured by the weight of your game bag, but in indelible memories that can be cherished forever.

COLORFUL COVEYS
My hunting years have always been painted in ecological colors.

In my early days, during bird season I'd hunt an old spur-line railroad while walking to school. Bobwhite quail were the only native upland game birds to hunt in northern Illinois, and a flush of quail didn't come often. But that didn't stop me from pursuing them with Mike, an untrained springer spaniel, even though the quail population did not decline because of our efforts. Those were memorable years, and certainly influenced the course of events later in my life.

Since then, I've been lucky enough to live most of my life in the shadow of the northern Rocky Mountain Front, where the High Plains slip downward toward the nation's breadbasket—out where there is no limit of how far you can walk or how far you can see. It wasn't long before two important elements emerged in my youth: the first was to have bird dogs surrounded by miles of unmolested country from horizon to horizon; the second was a covey bird called gray partridge or what we call Huns.

When I first started out, I'd drift for hours with my dogs across the immense space under the vault of the Montana sky. And after sizing up the big open prairie I realized there was a lot to learn about Huns and the world around them, so my goal was to stay riveted to the real business at hand. First and foremost, I started keeping daily, detailed field notes throughout the year on every aspect of Hun behavior. Each year I gained more knowledge and skill about where and how to find them. That became a successful strategy and remains an ongoing learning process even to this day.

Over this same period I began developing my own hard-charging Brittany bloodlines for the sole purposes of hunting Huns in big, open country. Like me, over time the dogs no longer wasted motion in unproductive areas and they fine-tuned their skills for finding and holding birds. But no matter how many times I have gone afield, the best Hun hunting stories grow out of the face of the land. A frost initiates the serene death of the green hues and increases a spectrum of color values. It isn't really quality Hun hunting until the country becomes ablaze with red, orange and yellow.

I have been hunting for several weeks, but on this day, winter seems to advance closer. Storm clouds hang over the distant mountains, carrying a moist aroma. I park the hunting rig off the dirt road that crosses the small earthen dam. Once the dogs are on the ground a pair of widgeons wing off the pothole edged in ice.

With a gentle wind on my face and the lack of green vegetation, the scenting condition fuels the dogs' desire to hunt. Sure of my destination, I climb a steep incline, top the ridge, and survey the panoramic view of Earth's uplifts and mountains formed from tectonic forces. I know this land, and every landmark is anchored in my mind. The dogs cross the parched grassy slope that feeds precious spring water to the wide draw below. At one point, the draw abruptly narrows and descends over a rocky sandstone wall; the dogs have been here before and look for water below the dry waterfall.

Most years there are four to five coveys of Huns that live between the high ridge and the riparian draw. But this season I know the whereabouts of only two coveys that reside here. I cannot see them, but they are there.

I pick my way down the talus slope, trying not to go too fast and lose my footing. Halfway down, the ground folds and a small rise obscures the dogs from view. As I move steadily up the easy grade, the far slope across the draw slowly comes into view again. As I top the low fold, Winston is lock-up pointing in the bottom of the draw. The other two dogs are strung out holding solid between Winston and me. Nothing moves as I slowly descend toward the first two dogs. Winston is facing me at the far edge of an alizarin crimson patch of cover. Sensing the covey is between us, I slowly walk in.

The flush is picture perfect. There is a whirl of wings and the 28-gauge side-by-side comes up quickly and a single Hun tumbles to the ground. Relaxed, I fix my eyes on the rest of the covey as they turn, cross the drainage, and land above a rocky outcropping of myriad lichen colors, their small silhouettes catching the low ambient light. Upon landing, the birds scurry up the grassy hillside out of sight. There's no need to hurry.

LESSONS LEARNED
Dave Sheley

I'm driving down the long road that Ben calls his driveway and I am thinking back to the first time I spoke with him. The ad had said "order here or call" for a copy of Ben's book *Winston*, about one of his great Brittanys. I could not believe that Ben answered the phone when I called. I ordered the book, however the pressing question wasn't when it would arrive but "Could you please give me some advice on hunting Montana Huns and, more importantly at the time, sage grouse?" He was very helpful, yet being the good teacher that he is, he didn't give me all the answers, just a solid base from which to work.

I did a lot of walking that first year and learned a great deal but didn't have much bird contact. I managed to get my first sage grouse, but that was about it. The second year, though, after talking to Ben some more and with lessons learned from the first hunt, we had a much more enjoyable conversion and the start of a deeper friendship. Phrases like "I get it now," "we were in birds most of the time," and "I got my trophy mount for my gun shop" were my report.

The truck bounced off the boulder-sized rock on the road—Ben will smile and say that it keeps the riffraff out and everyone else slowed down—which brings me back to the present. I am going to meet Ben for the first time! My wife and I and our three children were vacationing by Yellowstone. I called Ben before we left Minnesota to ask if I could come by and buy him lunch. He said,

"No, you are not buying me lunch, but you can run dogs with me." I about dropped the phone, I was so excited. He said to bring the family and that Bobbie could take them on a hike while we are out. I must have made a good impression on him, because we were supposed to be back around noon and we didn't get back until three-thirty, much to the chagrin of my waiting family.

Now the phone calls are more frequent. We talk about birds, doubles and dogs. I gave him a beautiful pointer pup last year. My son and I go fly fishing with him each spring. I stop to see him every fall. I know some things about him that you might not. His middle name is Oswalt. Bobbie, his wife, is an absolute gem. His favorite hunting dog is the English Pointer, and his favorite game birds are pheasants. Okay, so I lied about the last two "facts."

Ben has taught me so much about Huns, sage grouse and fly fishing. Most importantly, Ben has taught me to share. Share what you know and love. Fishing with him is talking with a fly rod in my hand and hunting is walking with a side-by-side in my hand and bird dogs on the ground. Talking about past hunts, old dogs and even older shotguns. He will always be a whisper in my ear when I'm on the prairie; now, my next hunt and forever. I can only hope someday, someone hears my voice in their ear.

HIGH PLAINS LOWDOWN
Head for the West's High Plains, where you'll find
sharp-tailed grouse memorable.

Say "sharp-tailed grouse" to an old sodbuster and he'll tip back his wear-stained, weathered, wide-brim Stetson, spit out a chew of Copenhagen, look you in the eye and then to the hills and ask if you mean "wild chickens." The name "wild chickens" was a generational hand-me-down to describe the three species of prairie grouse that were once numerous across the High Plains of North America. For old-timers, chickens were not considered a hunter's sport, but a meal on the table to break the monotony of salt pork and beans. Like fresh dandelion greens and gooseberry pie, "wild chickens" were seasonal, still dressed in pinfeathers and plinked with a .22 rifle. Mention sharp-tailed grouse to new-age bird hunters, and they immediately identify it as the most abundant grouse spread over a huge area west of the Mississippi. To this day, much of that country remains as wild as the bird.

Sharp-tailed grouse, also known simply as sharptails, followed the plow westward, survived the market hunter, and have filled the niches of the other two prairie grouse (greater and lesser prairie chickens). They are one of the few game birds to have taken advantage of physical changes in the landscape. The strength of these great game birds is their adaptability to live in just about every type of cover. Sharptails are found in agricultural holdings, plains grasslands, shrub grasslands, intermountain grasslands, cut-over woodlands, and forest burns. Not only have they adapted to major changes in the environment; they also thrive on a wide variety of foods.

Sharp-tailed grouse are less predictable to hunt than most other game birds. Their movements are more erratic and they need more cruising space than smaller game birds. Although the birds are non-migratory, their daily and seasonal shifts can be extensive. During the early fall, sharptails are in small family flocks and are less mobile; but as the season progresses, being a gregarious bird, they begin to congregate in larger and larger groups and travel farther seeking out new or different food sources. Later in the season, it can be said, they are birds of "here today, gone tomorrow."

Some of my favorite sharptail hangouts are made up of grassy hills with riparian drainages choked with fruit-laden shrubs, abandoned homestead surrounded by shelterbelts, and large stubble grain fields with grassy drainage draws.

Here are a couple of descriptive places that I frequent during the sharptail hunting season:

There are several large parcels of land, on the face of Montana, where I hunt that have changed very little through the years and where it seems time has stood still. One such place is a large ranch that I've hunted for years. That started when the rancher drew a map... with his boot... in the dirt... next to a feedlot... to show me the exact location of a brushy riparian coulee where a bunch of young sharptails spooked the rancher's horse during a cattle roundup. The dirt map is still vivid in my mind and is as reliable for hunting as it was on the day the dogs and I first set foot in the coulee.

Another favorite area I've hunted for decades is a true model of supreme sharp-tailed grouse habitat. This scenic thousand-acre high-tabled benchland is bisected by a wide, deep riparian coulee. Perpendicular to the coulee fingerlike grassy draws reach into flat tableland. Each year, one side of the coulee is planted in wheat, while the other side lies fallow. Then the planting process is reversed, creating a continuous yearly winter food source for wildlife.

Now an interlude: It was midmorning when I parked the hunting vehicle in the shadow of the haystack. In the distance, low, dark clouds spilled over the mountains, sweeping in moist air. I uncased my lightweight 28-gauge side-by-side, stuffed several shotshells in my bird-hunting vest, and released the three dogs from their compartments.

I struggled while opening the barbed-wire gate as it was wide enough for a 24-foot combine to go through. Then I walked the field along the edge of a coulee so I could scan the complete panoramic view and still observe the dogs reaching out in stubble far ahead. Periodically, the dogs would disappear in a grassy draw that drains spring run-off into the riparian coulee. With a moist, cool breeze moving across the golden harvested wheat field, scenting conditions could not have been better for the dogs. It wasn't long before one locked up and found the birds.

On the face of the High Plains, there are many such places to hunt. Take the essential first step on the sharptail journey, that all-important building block for success, and plan a hunt on the High Plains.

RENAISSANCE MAN
Ryan Petrie

I've been privileged to accompany Ben O. Williams on scores of adventures over the years, from hunting quail in New Mexico to Huns in Montana and fishing classic rivers of the West. But my most memorable and personal time spent with Ben occurred when just the two of us hopped into his Tundra—distinguished by the personalized HUNS 1 license plate and custom dog carrier, it is one of Montana's singular vehicles—and simply drove around Livingston on a rainy afternoon.

He showed me the school where he taught for many years while also serving as football and basketball coach. Along the way we stopped by numerous places in town where his beautiful sculptures were displayed as well as homes he had designed.

To finish our trip, Ben stopped and introduced me to a couple fishing stretches on the Yellowstone River with little-known access that made them undiscoverable to the nonresident.

The little journey broadened my view of a man I had associated with hunting, fishing, comradery, expertly prepared meals, and, of course, those wonderful dogs. Now I also know him as a teacher, sculptor, an architect, author and selfless mentor. What a rich life! What priceless memories he has given me.

For that and more, Ben, I thank you.

PRAIRIE BOOMERS

*Season in and season out, this Western game
bird fuels my hunting passion.*

Again I travel east, over a blue highway passing through big, open grasslands that stretch for miles. To my left, the mixed grass prairie extends north through much of the Dakotas and south through most of Nebraska, Kansas and Oklahoma. On this tranquil autumn day, the golden grassy hills seem to roll like vast ocean waves ahead of my pickup. All around me I see reminders of the first place I hunted greater prairie chickens, an event that has stayed in the back of my mind ever since. They've become an historical romance and a legendary game bird in my life.

No other game bird has given a greater charm to the prairies than the prairie chicken. No sound ever had more feeling or remembered resonance than the early morning booming that flows from a high hill close to a homestead, or a distant knoll above a ranch house.

No doubt, this country also stirs my memory—this land that's been accommodating to millions of prairie chickens, that through the centuries has attracted imperiled homesteaders living off the land, and hosted market hunters who barreled, boxed and shipped thousands upon thousands of birds to the large population centers across the United States. Back then, the prairie chicken was the people's bird—belonging to the ranch hand, the farmer who toiled in the field and the town and city folk. The bird had no rival in popularity; yet, it came and went with the sodbusters.

Although the prairie chicken adapted to the changing conditions, it could not endure the destruction of most of its range. So great was the loss of prairie habitat that only a few states still have the true, large, open areas needed for the birds' survival. It is these mixed prairie grasslands, properly managed, that furnish the cover vital to their nesting, roosting and booming grounds.

Thankfully, today I can still hunt one of the finest game birds ever to cross in front of the barrels of my smoothbore. Having breakfast in a small town café, a friendly farmer/auctioneer seated next to me suggested I meet his friend. He said, "John knows more about old farm machinery, and prairie chickens, than anyone around. Go see him, I'm sure he would rather talk chickens than work." Unlike most of the old family homesteads, John's place never passed back into government public grasslands.

It was midmorning the day I first met John Larson (not his real name), wearing patched bib overalls and standing next to a line of old vintage tractor parts. I introduced myself and then explained the reason for the visit.

John half-smiled, and introduced himself in return: "Now, you want chickens, not grouse?" he asked. "You want them barred, the ones with yellow feet?"

I nodded in agreement.

Drawing bird-location maps in the dirt and telling hunting stories came easily for John. Looking toward the grassland, he pointed, and then looked at his watch.

"Well," he said, "I see you have some bird dogs. Just take them toward those low hills and hunt the sunny side. Chickens like being in the sun late morning so they should be there by now." Then, he said, "It's time for you to get going."

I thanked him for the help and left.

I had the pleasure of knowing John for some years before he died. In conversations, he taught me a lot about old yellowlegs. Nowadays, after I turn off the blue highway and continuing past John's homeplace, his knowledge and memory pop into my imagination. For two miles, the golden mixed prairie grass is swirling in back of me. I park in the same spot where years ago John instructed me to start.

Outside of my hunting rig, the sweet smell of dry forbs and prairie grass flows across the landscape. Geared up with dogs ready, I walk toward the distant higher ground. After some time, I arrive at the base of the hills. Halfway up the gradual slope, both dogs slow and then lock on point. As I move slowly up the incline, two birds, dark against the hill, flush beyond shotgun range, swing past me, and sail down the slope.

As I continue walking up, the prairie explodes, the sky filling with chickens. At that moment I remember what John had said to me years ago: "No bird has thrilled a hunter more than a prairie chicken flushing out from under a dog's nose... and the rest of the flock getting up in all directions."

At day's end, driving past John's old family homestead, I have a strong feeling: I will always be thankful for what John taught me about hunting prairie chickens.

KNOWING THE GREAT PLAINS
Hailey Wilmer

Every great bird hunting story takes place on some strategically anonymous patchwork of prairie or farm ground. You know the place. That secret spot where eons of geology, climate and evolution come together with more recent human decisions about land use: plowing, grazing, haying, permission. In the short term, the story depends on the birds' response to weather, ecology, time of day; the dogs' heart and lungs and know-how; and whatever instinct or experience or dumb luck pulls you, the hunter, to walk one side-hill or draw or meadow and not another.

Finally, in the sharp sideways December light and a sharper wind comes the instant and infinite crux of the day, a remembering and forgetting of it all, all at once. The world stops cold as the red and white Brittanys lock up on a point and back. A few steps forward. Raise your shotgun with the rusty-gate squeak of wings through still air. Keep your head down, swing through, and the Hun drops in the grass. Before your ears register the shots fired, the dogs lunge ahead to find the bird, and the word rushes back to motion. If you're lucky, or Ben Williams, you might even shoot a double.

Ben is neither the first nor the last to make prairie both stage and talent in his writings. In Rolvaag's *Giants in the Earth* (1924) the prairie is antagonist and killer. In Galvin's *The Meadow* (1992), it is 360 acres of unforgiving toil, isolation and struggle, a place shared but "never owned" by so many work-calloused souls over the years. In the arc of our relationship with these "lands that hold the world together," as Thad Box would say, we have feared and lost to the harsh climates of the prairies, but we have also conquered and vanquished.

The push to innovate and produce has left just a fraction of the native prairies throughout the Great Plains unturned. Geographer Nathan Sayre argues that the prairies and rangelands that persist to provide habitat for upland bird and other species, do so because we have not (yet) figured out how to turn them into something else more profitable. But by putting the prairies on a shelf, to preserve, as if in a picture frame, some iconic pre-European version of the world that would never have existed without human-set fires and massive herds of large herbivores, we also fail the prairies. They cannot be locked in time. Now, they depend upon our decision making, knowledge and management. Research has slowly caught up to what Ben and other hunters, managers and conservationists have seen firsthand—that the resilience of prairies as complex ecosystems requires adaptive management for diverse patterns and processes across scales, and that this management depends upon the knowledge, networks and stewardship of people, collaborating across viewpoints and objectives, who live in and know the prairies.

It is easy to get nostalgic about bird hunting and all it entails: the old English shotguns and comradery, and the traditional glass of single malt scotch at day's end. Ben loves all of that. But he is not really nostalgic. He knows, from the six or more decades he has chased the critters up the wind-swept hills of Montana and elsewhere, that bird hunting, and birds, depend on forward thinking. Ben could easily pass for a Millennial if the evidence were energy and curiosity, except that he is in his mid-eighties, and remembers a time before agriculture industrialization and a development boom took turns depopulating and repopulating the plains. In all that time he has learned to think, and teach, ahead.

Every time I talk to Ben he has a new batch of puppy "employees" on the way, or another young hunter to mentor. Why? He knows that we can do better. We can learn from our mistakes, learn to manage and maintain the complex prairies rather than fear, control and transform them. And if you follow Ben, he will show you his way to learn the prairies: by being out on them, in them, because of them. Every day, every month, for years, refining that decision point where geology, evolution and climate taper down to a single morning in a particular pasture, with plan and a dog, and a point, and a shot.

ROARING SHADOWS

*When hunting the High Plains, a memorable day afield
will include our largest grouse—the greater sage.*

I love a fast-and-furious day of hunting Hungarian partridge, but there are times when a desire comes to travel through shrub grasslands in the shadow of the Rocky Mountain range to hunt the largest native North American game bird species, the greater sage grouse. Called the "cock of the plains" by members of the Lewis and Clark Expedition, greater sage grouse were once the most plentiful game birds on the High Plains.

Maybe it's the habitat in which they live or maybe it's the wildness of the birds themselves, but both seem prehistoric. Sage grouse are special and hunting them with pointing dogs is a true pleasure because they give off a tremendous amount of scent and they flock up, sometimes forming groups of thirty birds. Once flushed, their whirring wings over a sea of sage cast shadows on the prairie. When these big grouse fill the sky, and when one is brought back to the earth, you've taken a true trophy, with memories of a passing time and a historic place.

Keep in mind that hunting these birds is a special opportunity and is completely different than any other bird hunting. The Montana season runs from September to November 1, and on the eastern side of the Missouri River in Montana, where there is a vast swath of Bureau of Land Management public access, there is still a good population of these birds.

More years ago than I care to remember, I saw my first sage grouse of the season as I was glassing a large sagebrush flat looking for mule deer. Back then, sage grouse were mysteries to me. I knew them as residents of miles of purple sage, places with no fences where homesteaders passed up settlement because they could not make a living in such arid country. Even back then, despite game management and research efforts by state and federal wildlife biologists that date back years before I witnessed my first big grouse on the Western plains, sage grouse populations were on the decline in some states. Still, I found them to be big, enchanting birds.

Unlike most other upland game birds, sage grouse are completely dependent year round on a single type of plant. The birds need expansive areas with good high-winter sagebrush cover, good spring nesting habitat, and a community of green forbs and insects within the shrub grassland. But as with so many threatened and endangered species, it's not the decline of the animals, but the demise of the species' ecosystem that is the problem today.

Despite habitat disruption and population declines, sage grouse can still be hunted in the fall in several Western states. I suggest that if you do consider hunting North America's largest grouse, treat them as special and trophy birds—which means taking one is enough, in my opinion.

This year's moisture proved helpful for the young grouse and the population exploded. Call them what you like, but when hunting Bill Landers' place in Montana, we called them "thunder chickens." Landers, the rancher, told me that every morning and early evening the birds would pour into the alfalfa to feed on the new growth after the second cutting. Driving to his ranch and seeing a hundred birds in the meadow was not unusual. We first caught sight of them in the alfalfa surrounded by miles of shrub grasslands. Sage grouse were everywhere and the dogs filled their nostrils with the lovely scent.

Bill's place is situated in rugged, strong and unforgiving country. It sits in the shadow of the Rocky Mountain range, where Chinook winds and thunderstorms roll across the landscape, unexpectedly appearing and disappearing like the thunder chickens themselves. These magnificent birds and the Rocky Mountain land they occupy embody a magic that's inexpressible.

There is no need for an exclusive sage grouse hunting trip. If you're planning a hunting trip for other Western game birds in the vicinity of sage grouse living space, I highly recommend pursuing them. It is well worth the effort and it takes you into country not shared by many. The country, like the bird, is big, wide and handsome. The sight of 10 or 20 large, black-and-white prairie bombers catapulting into the sky all at once, cutting past you and feathering the wind overhead, will get your undivided attention. Just seeing the "cock of the plains" airborne is a memorable experience, whether you kill one or not.

The days of the big grouse hunts, once common, are now waning; but there is still time for a sporting connection to be made. I'll close with a capsule of a hunt from my diary in early September many years ago:

The sky darkened and closed over the higher peaks, but there was little rain. Several miles down the highway, the sun had come out and the black-top intersecting Powder Basin looked much as it had in midsummer. Every day, thunderstorms formed over the mountains dumping sheets of rain across the vast landscape of Powder Basin.

Hunt for these big, magnificent grouse. You'll treasure the experience and their landscape.

NOT A DOG PERSON
Kirby Hoyt, Vintage Doubles

My wife's daughter and her husband and new baby recently have come to live with us as they relocate to our fair city. Darla and I have been living here for the past dozen years or so and it was somewhat of an eye opener to have our house increase in occupancy from our little family of two humans and three canines.

Darla's daughter quickly noted several aspects of our dogs' behavior and our behavior towards our dogs. The first full day here she said, "Why don't you keep them outside?" My immediate response (within) was this obviously is not a dog person. On the second day, Lacy said, "Why do you have dogs?" This said with the aplomb that from her point of view, having dogs was almost like some form of self-flagellation. I think she would prefer forty days in the desert and maybe some stigmata spikes to having dogs... Again, I held my tongue but immediately confirmed my first impression: This is not a dog person.

Then, in an almost Zen epiphany, I was able to see what Lacy was seeing, the view from an outsider of our living environment and the interactions of the mammals within it. I believe something that made an impression the first day of her family's arrival was how we talked to our animals and they just looked at us and did not respond, unless we raised and deepened the throat of our requests. We would apologize for the jumping up on crotches and car doors, but it was obvious we put up with some pretty irritating behavior.

Two of our three dogs are French Brittanys, not especially large dogs; in fact, considered rather small for a hunting breed. It never ceases to amaze me how they can remove any form of food from a kitchen counter. Never in front of you, but you only have to turn your back for a micro second and glance back to see on fully extended hind legs, a dancing ballerina Brittany helping him or herself to some lovely kitchen morsel. This has been a whole prime rib. The week our house guests arrived it was a whole cherry pie.

Then there is the matter of the kitchen garbage can. It has a pedal to be pushed to open it for quick disposal—human mammals use it for disposal, that is. Our canine mammals quickly discovered that the pedal could be pushed to retrieve tasty snacks; the snacks, like forbidden fruit, all the more tasty as they know we don't want them to have them. Or, perhaps that is not it at all. Maybe they are looking at us in pure disgust as they watch us throw away perfectly wonderful food!

After many attempts to train them to stay out of the garbage pail, I had an idea. I took eight or so extremely sharp Sheetrock screws and screwed them through the lid of the hinged garbage can. Visualize the open mouth of the can like that of a great white shark. I was so proud of my accomplishment, but after a test period I had to remove the screws. They did not deter our crafty canine mammals, who found a way to delicately hold the lid open and pick out the refuse without being disturbed by the can's sharp teeth. I knew it was time to remove them when Lacy was disposing of some leftover food and came back to me with a bleeding hand...

Now back to where I started this romance. My stepdaughter comes into our world and sees dancing, food-snatching ballerina Brittanys behaving very badly. She sees expensive and mouthwatering food robbed from our counters and plates, she sees dog hair everywhere, remnants of ripped dog toys spread throughout the house. She finds the kitchen garbage spread over the floor. Putting myself in her shoes, I thought her response to our canine family perfectly reasonable, at least, from someone that is not a dog person.

What she does not "get" is why we put up with all this. We love our dogs, our dogs love us. An unconditional relationship that I would say is the norm between these two species of mammals, but a relationship that is so uncommon and rare between the humans themselves. She is not a dog person. No one is perfect.

THE SPANIEL YEARS
One breed of bird dog has been a thread woven through the author's life.

My first dog was a springer spaniel given to me when the dog was two years old. Mike was his name but I sometimes called him Mike the Dog, to emphasize to schoolmates I personally had a bird dog of my own. His puppy years were spent in a large city, with little space for a dog of his pedigree to run. I was a country boy living in a perfect place for a dog of this caliber.

He soon showed such a remarkable talent for hunting that I amused myself trying to train him. Often I would play "hide and seek" with him in the big, open woods. With such willingness and energy, how he enjoyed the lessons seeking me out!

I had no dog training experience, it just happened, and there blossomed out of it a wonderfully close-working relationship. We were beginners, both experimenting with the unfamiliar and both so eager to discover bird hunting. With my lack of hunting knowledge, Mike used his biological instincts and worked hard to seek out game birds. We hunted the crop fields, fence rows, and brier tangles adjacent to the abandoned spur-line railroad tracks.

One day, walking an untidy shucked cornfield, Mike worked a few yards ahead of me, covering every likely holding spot where a pheasant could hide. As we arrived at the end of the field, there was an explosion of catapulting pheasants flushing in all directions. I realized then that having a good bird dog contributed a great deal to my hunting enjoyment. In my eyes, Mike was nearly perfect. A boy doesn't forget that sort of association.

When the season opened, I introduced Mike to the real purposes of bird hunting. However, upon my first shot fired, to my chagrin Mike displayed gun-shyness and ran straight home. Let me admit, I had no idea what to do. I was heartbroken and with such devotion toward Mike, I refrained from reloading the shotgun and headed home myself, hoping to ease his fear. Mike was sitting on the back porch and seemed hesitant at first, but then came bounding to me with loyalty and affection.

I realized the great responsibility of dog ownership and how important it was on my part to give Mike every opportunity to overcome his gun-shyness. Ultimately, with patience and persistence on my part, and with such a strong hunting desire on Mike's part, he conquered gun-shyness. In later days, he trusted the gun and recognized its purpose, which gave him the opportunity to capitalize on another strong biological gift—the ability to retrieve.

One afternoon, we went for a long hunt and were about to turn for home when Mike became greatly excited approaching a large patch of chokecherries along a wide overgrown fencerow. I did nothing and said nothing while he raced around and around. It all happened in a split second and before I had time to think, a large covey of bobwhite flushed high overhead. Being a novice hunter, I thought it was an impossible shot for me. But after the loud report, feathers drifted down and Mike jumped skyward, catching the dead quail in midair. He then turned to look at me, wagging his short tail, as if to say, "How about that retrieve!" Days like these strengthened our partnership.

Mike would never let on to being sore or tired from hunting

too long; nor was he bothered about unpleasant weather while in the field. Mike just didn't fuss and perhaps what he appreciated most was being able to hunt every chance he got with a trusted friend.

Owning a dog today is a lot different for me than it was when I was young. Back then, caring for a dog was simple. Dogs were fed scraps and leftovers. Most lived outside in a wooden barrel stuffed with straw, or on the back porch, or in a barn. Most dogs never saw the inside of a house, but Mike was the exception and became my full-time house companion.

Looking back, I always consider that my career as a dog person really started when I got Mike, who taught me a lot about dogs in general and how to hunt game birds. In return, I let him be what he was bred to be. To this day, every time I see a springer spaniel, Mike shines bright in my memory.

The American Brittany, now called the Brittany in the United States, once carried the name "Brittany Spaniel." For more than a half century, I have owned some astonishing bird dogs and most have been Brittanys. You can drop the word "spaniel" from the dog, but you can't take the innate spaniel characteristics out of the breed. For me, the word spaniel still runs deep in my line of bird dogs—and in my affection for them.

FRIENDS IN THE FIELD
Roger Catchpole

I wasn't meant to get a puppy. My wife wanted a baby. However, a grand bargain was reached and a cocker spaniel arrived. We named him Austin Powers on account of him being English, red in color, and a larger than life character. He was our international man of mystery.

At twelve weeks of age he was already a bundle of love and desire. And, while a little hairier than our intended child, Austin soon found his corner in our home and a place in our hearts. By twelve months he had developed into a dynamic bird finder.

Having left England years earlier, I enjoyed Austin's daily reminder of home. Our family lived in Florida, which provided a contrasting experience to our lives in rural England. And while Austin adapted fast, my own adjustment took longer. In his first season Austin hunted mourning doves at my local dove club and wood duck on my friend's farm. Hunts we both remember fondly. Certainly, these early experiences gave Austin a hunger for the hunt that has never since waned.

As I write, Austin sits by my desk. He rests, all the while anticipating the call to arms. For that reason, he never lets me out of his sight lest I abandon him to hunt alone. Once I left home to catch an early morning flight to hunt with Ben in Montana only to receive a panicked call from my wife requesting help to console our distraught boy. Austin knew I'd packed my hunting gear and couldn't understand why I'd left him.

On our first trip away together we travelled to Georgia, where Austin was introduced to gentleman Bob. The hunt was something neither of us will ever forget. Since the moment he flushed that first rise of quail he has been a covey bird fanatic. A passion we share.

Following our move to New England, Austin has progressed to hunting pheasants, chukar, woodcock and ruffed grouse. However, quail remain his true love. I've also promised Austin a Hun hunt with Ben, and I'm certain he won't forget.

Never a day goes by when Austin isn't a tail-wagging bundle of canine joy. He's a great bird dog, but more importantly he's a loved family member. Austin is also now a proud puppy brother to baby Rose. So I guess I've fulfilled the grand bargain.

Although Austin is still young, I know that day will come. I've lost dogs before, some through old age others in their prime, but this will be different.

Until then, I am thankful. Thankful we have this time together. Thankful we can chase birds afield, as friends.

MY ALPHA BRITTANY
Michael McGillicuddy always figured it out.

It all started in the early 1950s. Back then, English pointers were the preferred bird dogs south of the Mason-Dixon Line, English setters were the grouse dogs of the North Country, and both breeds were well established and the hunters' choice for upland game birds in North America. Never having owned a pointing breed, it seemed to me at the time that the English setter would best fit my needs for hunting upland game birds in Middle America. But that didn't happen.

Before I could locate an English setter pup, an unfamiliar breed came into my life—the Brittany spaniel. Some hunting folks said these dogs were mutts and had no noble field bloodlines. Little did they (or I) know what a great companion and bird-finding machine this French import would be. Call the dogs what you like (as associations have juggled the breed's name a bit over the decades), but they got in the way of my selection of a "classic" pointing dog.

Oddly enough, the Brittany came into my life in an unusual way. While I was attending college, the name of a dog breeder surfaced who happened to live in town. I was informed that Oberlin Kennels had English setter pups, but it turned out that the owner raised Brittany spaniels, which at the time were fairly new to North America. Loving springer spaniels since boyhood, I found the word "spaniel" interwoven with a pointing breed captured my undivided attention.

During my college years, I worked for Oberlin Kennels. Walter Oberlin presented me with the opportunity, the knowledge, and the gift of a lifetime. I became convinced that the establishment of Brittanys in North America was secure, and I became intensely interested in the breed.

After completing college, I moved westward to the High Plains, taking two female Brittanys with me. A pup I named Williams' Pride Michelangelo arrived by train a year later and became the male foundation of my own bloodlines. Michael McGillicuddy, or just Mike, was his field name—depending on if I had to add a little weight to him for a rabbit excursion.

My dog training method has always been modeled after what Walter Oberlin emphasized as being more instinctive than programmed. I do not look upon an animal as being a machine forced to perform particular duties that are not natural to a dog's behavior. I believe a dog should be allowed to have a bad day so that it can find out what works. With a bird dog, this requires a controlled hand and a neglected whistle. I have learned, "You have to let a dog be a dog and allow it to work out its own mistakes."

Michael McGillicuddy had some unique traits and field performances that indicated he was not exactly your typical bird dog. In fact, anyone who really understands gun dogs would likely conclude that his modest disposition would not make him a strong-going pointer or retriever. The fact is, despite such impressions, Mike's mild manners were deceiving and most folks who saw him work did not recognize his full potential. He had a medium range, but could go all day and was a persistent dead-bird hunter. He was spectacular at finding cripples, and he understood exactly how the whole program worked.

Mike's pointing ability was phenomenal and at times he seemed uncanny and almost humorous when retrieving. For example, one time I shot a Hun that plunged into a chokecherry thicket down a steep draw. He marked the downed bird perfectly. It was a very hot day and, after waiting for some time, I went looking for him. He had taken the dead bird in his mouth to a small creek below the thicket and was stretched out in the cool water. Upon seeing me, he made the retrieve, and then grinned happily at me.

Upland bird hunting with McGillicuddy was serious business, but the versatile waterfowl stuff was more casual. He would crawl next to me if I were on a sneak up to open water while listening to vocal mallards, knowing exactly what I was doing. He loved water and approached it aggressively when going after a downed duck or goose.

Duck hunting was over one day and I was carrying a limit of mallards toward the VW bug when a snipe flushed. I automatically shot, and McGillicuddy found and retrieved it. After that, he began hunting and pointing snipe. I have no idea how many times I walked past snipe spots while hunting ducks, but once I shot the first one he had no difficulty in sorting out their scent.

Some might have called McGillicuddy a bit laid-back and too small to head up my generations of bird dogs. But he fathered my bloodline of Brittanys, which produced much bigger, bolder, rangier, field-smart dogs, with good bird sense. McGillicuddy just figured things out.

ZEN MASTER
Tom Davis

After a long drive from Wisconsin, Terry Barker and I were cutting the dust at the Livingston Bar & Grille. The bartender, sizing us up as the sportsmen we imagine ourselves to be, asked, "You boys trout fishing?"

"Doing a little bird hunting," Terry replied.

"Hmmm," the guy mused, wiping a Pilsner glass with a bar towel. "You've got your work cut out for you. From what I've heard the birds are down this year."

I sipped my martini, smiled knowingly, and said, "We're hunting with Ben Williams."

"Oh!" the barman said, visibly impressed. "That's different. If you're hunting with Ben you'll do fine. He knows the location of every covey within a 50-mile radius—and his dogs are the best in the country."

Ben Williams' reputation, as they say, precedes him. And having had the pleasure and privilege of hunting with Ben and his "pack" of Brittanys and pointers several times over the years, let me assure you that this reputation is fully deserved. He never hurries, he never yells, he never worries when the occasional covey busts wild, and on the rare occasions when you can twist his arm into carrying a scattergun he almost never misses.

And yes, he does seem to know the location of every covey of Huns and sharptails within a 50-mile radius.

In short, Ben makes it all look as effortless as water flowing through a Paradise Valley spring creek. I've come to think of him as the Zen Master of Upland Bird Hunting.

Perhaps the most remarkable thing about hunting with Ben is how utterly relaxed he is once he turns loose his dogs—never fewer than four and sometimes as many as eight! It's that Zen thing. He hardly ever calls to them, and while he carries a whistle I can't swear I've ever seen him take it from his shirt pocket.

Once in a while he'll mock-scold "Get over here, ya varmint," but everyone, including the dog, knows he's only half-serious. All of his dogs are roamers—they have to be to find birds in the big country he hunts—and when he wants one to check in he'll hit the "page" button on his e-collar transmitter and pretty soon the dog he's looking for will come galloping over the hill.

Here's a mind-blowing glimpse into Ben's world. The *come* command, for all intents and purposes, is the only formal command his dogs know. At some point after hunting with him for a while it occurred to me that I'd never heard him utter that most ubiquitous (and overused) of pointing dog commands, *whoa*. When I asked Ben if he teaches it he shrugged and said, "I could—but there's no real reason to."

In other words, he doesn't need to tell his dogs to stand still. When it's time to stop, they know it.

As Ben puts it in his book *Bird Dog: The Instinctive Training Method*, "I feel over-training and using too many training aids can prevent a dog from fully developing his natural instincts... Using common sense and the simplest possible form of communication is the easiest way for both the dog and owner to achieve excellence."

I remember Ben helping me put this wisdom into practice with one of my own dogs. Ernie, an English setter, was in his second season—and he was a handful. I was uptight about running him with Ben's veteran dogs, fearful that he'd bust birds, steal points and generally be a royal pain in the ass. But Ben counseled me to take it easy and stay out of Ernie's way.

"His instincts are good," Ben said. "You watch: He'll figure it out."

As always, Ben's analysis was spot-on. When the opportunity arose, Ernie backed Ben's dogs as if he'd been doing it all his life—and when he slam-dunk pointed a big covey of Huns all on his own, I felt like I needed someone to grab my ankles and bring me back down to earth.

Ben just smiled and said, "What'd I tell you?"

THINKING OF WINSTON
The life of a traveling gun dog.

I wrote a book about my Brittany named Winston and our travels together and how he pointed all of North America's 18 major upland birds, from Alaska to Mexico. My interest in Brittanys started all the way back in the early 1950s with a dog named McGillicuddy.

Some say a man only deserves one great dog in a lifetime and great pointing dogs do not come along often. But I believe if you start with good bloodlines on both sides of the chain-link fence, and have a kennel of high-performance dogs for half a century, the chance of hunting with great dogs comes along more often. McGillicuddy, Leo, Shoe, Winston, Winston II, Hershey, Gina, Daisy, Chantilly—they were all great-performing gun dogs. And at present, my female Petunia out of Winston II, and her son, Gilly, and daughter, Merri Merri, carry on the tradition.

Breeding hunting dogs requires a good deal of thought and serious consideration well in advance of the actual mating. My sole purpose as a breeder has been to have outstanding bird dogs for my own use and to enhance the quality of the breed for hunting in the big, open country of the West (certainly not for capital gains). Chantilly, a hard-changing Brittany, whelped three litters, all sired by Shoe. Winston was the only pup I kept out of her last litter. As a pup, he disliked being alone, so I took him with the other 12 kennel dogs during field-running sessions.

At a young age, Winston became extremely independent, but

not competitive. He honored his kennelmates and never broke point until the birds flushed.

Early in his first summer, Winston made his first solid point and then began finding his share of birds. Later, as a young dog, chasing rabbits and other furry critters was not part of his teenaged agenda. Winston's purpose in the field seemed to be pursuing birds, and he was drawn to them like a magnet.

Winston had an aloofness about him. At home, he never demanded attention, but I always felt his presence, and he seemed to know I liked him close by. One day, while running hard in a large field of crested wheatgrass, Winston inhaled several weed seeds and a few days later developed a serious lung infection. After he spent three days with the veterinarian, my wife Bobbie brought him home and nursed him back to good health. He then became a permanent house companion. But as long as I can remember, one or two of the kennel dogs have always become house dogs.

Some folks believe a bird dog's performance is hampered or hindered if they live indoors. Having had both house and kennel dogs over the years, I have never found any difference in their performance and desire.

Winston was six months old when bird season opened in Montana. The season goes more than a hundred days and by the end, he had become an exceptional bird finder. At an early age, he became a big, strong-running male, with muscles of steel, and he seemed to float across whatever topography he was hunting. Day after day, even after low shadows crossed the landscape, he never showed signs of fatigue. When I returned to the hunting rig, bone tired, he'd make one last cast and invariably find and point another bunch of birds. Young Winston earned a favored priority as a hunting partner, and over the next few years we hunted every upland game bird in North America.

Winston covered thousands of miles, and together we hunted some places so remote that no other canine, other than a few Arctic wolves, ever crossed the same soft tundra landscape. He chased birds in parched desert moonscapes, wet rain forests, open grassland prairie, sagebrush flats, steep talus slopes, golden stubble fields, uncut standing corn and overgrown woodlots. We traveled by train, boat, car, pickup truck and aircraft large and small, seeking all species of upland game birds in their respective habitats across the continent.

I don't deny having a prejudice about my Brittanys, but I try not to become biased about individual dogs, even though I certainly had favorites. Winston was just that—a favorite. It's hard to imagine, but he started out in a hurry to become great. And looking back, there may have been a reason. Most Brittanys live 14 or 15 years. Winston died at just eight years, seven months, and a few days. He may have been the best bird dog a man ever owned and my field journal is crammed with notes on wonderful hunts we had together.

To this day, every once in a while, it's kind of nice to see one of his descendants pointing on a distant hill. I squint my eyes and pretend to see Winston locked up on a covey of Huns—the birds he loved to hunt the most.

THE VISIT; A CONVERSATION OVERHEARD IN THE DOG BOX AT BEN'S PLACE

Robert Siler

Bean: Hey guys, we're stopping! Abby, can you see anything?

Abby: Can't see a thing! But, I'm hungry and really need to pee. Hey, Robert's letting us out! He's with some Ole Man! Can you guys hear those dogs? Must be fifty coon hounds in there!

Maggie: I've seen that guy before. We came by here several dog-years ago.

Skunk: Hey, that's the guy whose picture was on those books Abby chewed up. He really looks a lot older in person!

Mary: Hey, maybe Robert is dropping Abby off here. He did say he was really tired of her chewing up the bedding and pooping in the dog box! See ya, Abby!

Abby: He wouldn't leave me here!

Mary: Would too!

Skunk: Shut up, you two! Abby, don't worry, none of these dogs have long tails! Look!

Bean: Robert says, "Dogs without long tails are cheaper."

Bee: Girls, girls, there is one with a tail! And he's a handsome thing, too! Hey, there, cowboy!

Maggie: Bee, take a cold shower! Remember the last time you got all romantic with that big, no-tail dog from Georgia? Frankly, I was a little embarrassed! We had to wait three dog hours before we could get back in the truck to go hunt.

Mary: Why does the Ole Man have so many dogs? He must be really rich to feed them all.

Bean: Maybe he sells the poop?

Maggie: Last time I was here, I got to see his shotguns. He's so poor all his guns are really old! They look 1,400 dog-years old! In fact, he can't even afford to buy full-sized shells!

Bean: He must spend all his money trying to feed those dogs.

Abby: I'm hungry! Can we not talk about food!

Skunk: C'mon, let's load up and go hunting!

Maggie: Hold on, Skunk. This Ole Man just loves dogs! One time he posed for a picture with that big, white, goat-looking dog! Nobody else would pose with her and risk losing a body part!

Bean: Don't make fun of goat-dog! She's all sweetie-pie around her owner, then she'll catch you behind some sagebrush and tear you up!

Maggie: You girls listen to me! Seventy dog-years ago, when I was a pup, Sadie, Pepper and Bell and I took a trip with Robert and Terry. We rode forever. Finally, Robert let us out in a horrible area! It had sand and sharp rocks and thorny grass and things that hurt your feet. It was hot and dry and there were no streams to jump in! We had to wear shoes! I'm not telling a lie! Robert and Terry had a book with the Ole Man's picture on the cover. It was full of pictures and maps and all kinds of information about how to find quail out there!

Abby: Quail don't live in places like that, Maggie! I'm hungry!

Maggie: They do too, Abby. They have quail that run like rabbits, quail that have funny little feathers on their heads, and quail that have dots all over them. They were all different, but they all smelled like quail. I'm telling you guys, you are so lucky we are heading there again and really get to stretch our legs! We should thank the Wise Ole Man because we could be back in North Carolina hunting soybean fields and busting through honeysuckle thickets and briars all day and not finding any birds!

Bee: It's all true, ladies! That Wise Ole Man is the reason we've spent our lives pointing sharptails, sage grouse, ruffed grouse, prairie chickens, chukar, Huns, spruce grouse, blue grouse, valley quail, mountain quail, scaled quail, Mearns' quail, Gambel's quail and western bobwhite quail!

Bean: What about those big red, white and green chicken-looking birds that live in ditches? Are we going to get to hunt them, too?

Bee: Whatever you do, don't mention them around the Wise Ole Man!

Abby: I'm hungry!

Bee: Oh, there's that cute, little, slick-coated, long-tailed boy. Look at the size of his front paws! The short-tail dog I "hooked up" with had small front paws—Hummm! "Over here, cowboy!"

Mary: Can we just go hunting? Bee, you are so embarrassing!

DOGS ON THE PRAIRIE
To the author, hunting prairie game birds without
pointing dogs is an empty exercise.

I'm in my hunting-gear and kennel building lacing up my boots with mother, Petunia, daughter, Merri Merri—both Brittanys—and Misty, a sleek little English pointer. The three are hurrying me along with woofs and groans. The kennel dogs recognize the ruckus and sound off in a coyote-cadence concert, pleading to join us. After I load the hunting gear, I release the dogs and with cries of victory they scrabble out and race for the truck. Like rodeo clowns circling a mean bull, they run around the pickup begging to be loaded in. What a bright, sunny September Montana morning!

It's almost 11 o'clock when I turn off the engine and step out of the pickup; I'm surrounded by distant mountains that glisten from last night's fresh snowfall. The ranchers have collected the cattle from the high hills, so the land now belongs to the dogs and me. All is quiet—until the dogs start clamoring in their truck kennel compartments, each one anticipating being first out.

This morning, I choose the three lovely girls to hunt first and they eagerly wait behind the hunting rig. I stuff a few 28-gauge shells into my vest pocket, slide the shotgun out of its cotton sleeve, and signal the girls that it's time to begin. I walk a few yards, turn back toward the howls of despair, and softly say to the other dogs still in their kennels, "Your turn will come."

Many years ago we bought a small place in the Montana country long before it was considered fashionable. Back then, big-game animals dominated hunters' life lists. Cow and sheep dogs were the canines of choice for the open range; it was unheard of to put down dogs like mine for the sole purpose of hunting prairie game birds.

When I arrived, my view of the country available to me took on a completely different meaning and developing bird dogs for the purpose of pursuing wild game birds in big grasslands became an obsession. This obsession changed how I traversed the landscape and transformed my thinking about how bird dogs should work the country.

Unlike hunting Eastern woodland habitat, I devised a different playbook for dogs hunting prairie game birds. The key was to develop big-running dogs that gracefully worked birds at great distances. Then with a series of sensitive relocating points, the dogs would cautiously close in on their quarry—whereupon I paid close attention to the dogs' body language and their movements, which alerted me to what the birds were doing. Once the dogs locked in a solid point, I knew the birds had slowed or stopped moving and were ready to flush. I believe that most bird dogs, given the chance, have the potential to become better hunters, depending on the amount of real field experience they receive. The more often dogs are in the field hunting wild birds, the sharper their innate abilities become, which brings out the best of their bloodlines. The majority of my dogs are so field-hardened that they do what is expected of them. Most of all, they want to hunt.

Over the years, I have found that hunting multiple dogs together complements each of their efforts, which contributes to the overall game plan and enjoyment of the hunt. Though I have Brittanys and pointers, my selection of the combination of dogs to put down in the field is not based on the breed, but on the kind of terrain I'm hunting. There are times, if conditions dictate, when putting four— or even more—dogs on the ground might work best. To me, the dogs are the essence of the hunt so why not put more dogs on the ground?

Because I keep a dozen or more dogs at all times, I've found certain canine combinations work best in bringing out each dog's specialty. However, the magic number that suits my hunting style is four dogs.

By running four dogs, I can use combinations that vary depending on the type of terrain being hunted. All my dogs learn early in life to back and honor a point, which is critical to my hunting method. After a covey of Hungarian partridge or a flock of prairie grouse bursts skyward, each dog then uses its greatest asset, which may be retrieving, locating singles, or marking birds down.

For the past half century, more than a hundred bird dogs have passed through my hands, and this experience has grounded me to the prairie. Which is why I say: Hunting the prairie without pointing dogs, to my mind, is an empty exercise.

PLANTING FOR LIFE
Craig E. Roberts

When I think of Ben O. Williams, my memory flashes back to mid-April 1996. Back then I was four years into developing winter cover habitat projects with fellow members under the banner of Pheasants Forever. Ben contacted me to ask if he could join us to take photographs while we planted a shelterbelt near Denton, Montana. He planned to prepare a photo essay for publication in the *Pheasants Forever Journal*. His photo essay, titled "Planting for Life," was published in the journal the following year. Ben's profound interest in upland game bird habitat and the work we were doing to enhance habitat in central Montana prompted him to consider developing tree and shrub plantings on his own property along the Yellowstone River east of Livingston. Our friendship grew during the next few years as Ben continued adding shrub plantings to his expanding wildlife cover projects.

Of course, one cannot truly acknowledge knowing Ben without being personally escorted to his kennels and introduced to his legendary Brittanys and English pointers. Perk, Hershey, Merri Merri, Mac, the list of names seems endless. And I have trouble confusing the names of my dogs long gone with the two I now hunt over.

Ben's kindness and generosity towards me and his love and affection for his dogs has been an inspiration for me over the many years I've known him. I recall early in our friendship grousing about one of my dogs not delivering birds to hand. Ben reflected a moment and his reply was to the point and classic: Is your dog having fun? Are you having fun? My answer, an obvious yes. He followed with, "Place your bird in your vest, praise your dog and enjoy the moment." That was many years ago. I've taken it to heart and am reminded of his wise counsel each time one of my dogs returns with a bird in mouth. Each day in the field behind one's dog is to be cherished. Thank you, Ben.

LUNCH AT DOLLY'S

Thumbing through my hunting journal sparks memories.

September, 45 years ago in the town of Twenty Mile in Powder Basin County (okay, not its real name), and I'm standing on an unpainted, planked floor, facing a bar with four stools arrayed in front of it.

Atop the bar sits a gallon jar of pickled eggs and a small wooden barrel of pickled pigs' feet. Over the bar, just beyond arm's reach, bags of potato chips are clipped to baling twine. Beyond that are a large upright cooler, a two-burner stove, a half dozen bottles of whiskey, and a cash register open as if waiting to be filled. Above the register is a chalkboard on which is handwritten BURGERS ONLY. The other three walls are covered with cardboard prints of the "Enchanted Northland" from Hamm's Beer with the slogan "From the Land of Sky Blue Water."

I'm at Dolly's Sagebrush Oasis. This is not the original bar, but a smaller building put into service after an electrical fire gutted the original Twenty Mile watering hole. Now seated, I'm waiting to be served. Next to me is a weathered Basque sheepherder who I know lives mostly in solitude and tends nomadic sheep on open range; he's holding a half-empty beer. There are two other customers against the wall seated at a small table having coffee. Both men work for the state highway department, maintaining the only paved road through Powder Basin.

Polishing the oak-framed, glass-front cooler is the proprietor, a stout woman, wearing a faded apron displaying MILES RANCH

SUPPLIES—which is the only other business in town. After some time and without looking up, she asks, "What will you have?"

"I'll have a burger and root beer," I answer.

She turns and looks straight at me. "The only soda pop we have is Pepsi," she calls out.

I smile and add, "That's fine."

In one magical motion, she opens the cooler, pushes a bottle of Pepsi to me, flips the burger on the hot grill, and yells "Onion?"

"Yes, ma'am," I answer. With precision, the sizzling burger along with a thick slice of onion is enclosed in a bun and placed on a paper plate. "That's a buck," she says. I put down four quarters and a dime.

After some time, a friendly looking ranch hand comes through the door, sits next to me, and orders a beer. Now, I'm between the sheepherder and the cowboy, facing the bartender and in the mirror I see the other two customers watching us. The road workers are dressed more like wranglers, the cowboy is dressed more like a log-ger, the sheepherder is dressed like he needs a bath, the proprietor (except for the carpenter's apron) looks like a barmaid, and I'm wear-ing a well-worn L. L. Bean hunting shirt. The cowboy smiles, sips his beer, and starts the conversation.

"Dogs in your rig, tells me you're looking for sage hens." The birds were called sage hens back then. "First time hunting this country?"

Finishing the delicious, inch-thick burger with a swallow of Pepsi, I answer, "Yes it is. Thought I'd give it a try."

"Working cattle the other day, around Coyote Creek, west of here, I put up a hundred birds," he elaborates.

"I've fished the creek and know the area. I just might go there, thanks."

There's a long pause, then the sheepherder breaks the silence.

"Sage chickens are just like my band of sheep, they roam all over," he says and taps his fingers on the bar, indicating he's ready for another beer. "Like to eat them?" he asks.

"I do, if fixed right," I answer.

"Well," he says, "I'll plink a young one for stew once in a while, but not the older ones."

Just then, one of the road workers drifts over after hearing our conversation and interrupts: "I'd hunt the big reservoir north of here if I were you. See grouse every time we go by there," he assures me and waves goodbye.

Dolly cuts in and says, "You don't have to go any further than beyond the schoolhouse to get a wagonload of sage hens."

Itching to leave, I stand, pull change from my pocket, slide it to Dolly, thank them for the information, and say, "Have a beer on me." As I exit, they wish me luck.

Back then, the topography was a sea of high plains and historical sagebrush, which spread out for miles; the big, beautiful grouse of Powder Basin were everywhere.

Today, Coyote Creek still holds brook trout, but the bar is gone, the one-room schoolhouse is boarded up, and the continuous sage cover, which was critical for holding large populations of grouse, is now broken. Because of this, I never hear talk of Twenty Mile or grouse hunting Powder Basin anymore.

GOTTA DOUBLE
Mike Janeczko

S omeone once told me, or perhaps I read it somewhere, that in order to broaden historical intellectual horizons, as well as keep up with the current times, a person should hunt and fish with someone older and someone younger. As I'm now just shy of three score and ten it is becoming more and more difficult to fulfill the former category than the latter. Thank God for modern medicine, which now can perform so many mechanical miracles that keep us old geezers in the field doing what we love to do.

One of the characters that happenstanced into my life in the most improbable of places was Mr. Ben O. Williams. Sort of like the collision between two pickup trucks at a section line crossroads in the deserted landscape of western Kansas, we met aboard a driftboat on the Flambeau River in "da nortwoods" of northern Wisconsin bobbing deer hair poppers for smallmouth bass and muskies. Every now and then your path collides with someone whom you've never met before, but yet feel like you've known all of your life. Such was the case that hot, humid summer day fishing with Ben.

The fishing, or should I say the catching, that day was kinda slow, which is a fishing guide's euphemism for it really sucked. So, of course, inevitably the conversation rolled around to, what else, bird huntin' and bird dogs. As it turns out, Ben and I had been chasing bobwhites in pretty much the same off the beaten path western high plains stomping ground for over thirty years without ever having that strange crossroads collision. Go figure. So, later that fall after a hunt or two together on the flatlands, Ben was gracious enough to invite me to his place up in western Montana to chase some sharptails and Hungarian partridge. Would I accept his invite? Are you kidding me? That is like getting an invite from St. Peter himself to come out and do a little Bible study with him and a few of his apostle buddies up Jerusalem way!

After making the northern pilgrimage to the hills outside Livingston from my home base in Colorado, I found myself ensconced next to Ben in the cab of his traveling dog kennel with two Brittanys, Gilly and Merri Merri, along with my trusty old golden retriever, Mac, bumbling along a potholed two track in the proverbial middle of nowhere that is western Montana. It is precisely at moments such as this, mesmerized by the surrounding magnificent mountain landscape, that I truly believe that sometimes you find yourself in the middle of nowhere and sometimes in the middle of nowhere you find yourself.

As we began what I consider to be the ultimate silent walking meditation that is Hun hunting in tens of thousands of acres, I figured that after doing the high plains forced march hunt with a bunch of young bucks, this experience was going to be a piece of cake. I thought to myself, heck, hunting with someone over ten years my senior, finally I will be able to keep up. Oh how wrong could I be! To say the least, Ben is the living personification of the old cliché "walking your wheels off." He proceeded to cruise effortlessly over hill and dale (mostly hill) as if propelled by some invisible hover board while simultaneously, miraculously, keeping track of no fewer than six far-ranging, white-and-liver-splotched, cruise missile–like, four-legged, whirling blurs of energy.

It didn't take long, just a few wheezing, panting, high-altitude miles or so, till we noticed that there was a rocket or two or three in our mobile arsenal that were visibly unaccounted for. After utilizing the collar-mounted sonar devices, a procedure not unlike tracking the ping generated by one of those black boxes they use to locate downed aircraft in uncharted waters, we crested one more hill and spotted at least three motionless white specks waaaay out on the distant horizon. I commented that we best be hustling up there quickly, but Ben assured me not to worry, we could stop for a leisurely lunch break if we so desired, as his Brittanys would hold a point like so many maverick stones until we made our way up there ("up" being the operative word).

He was right. When we arrived at the scene we of course got the usual canine over-the-shoulder glare that says, "It's about friggin' time you guys got here!" Being the benevolent gentlemanly hunting host that he is, Ben insisted that I be the one to stride past those beautifully synchronized scattered stones and have the honor of taking the first covey flush of the day. OK... no pressure there! Ha! Sort of like Arthur Fiedler stepping down from the conductor's podium at Symphony Hall in front of the Boston Pops, handing you the baton and saying, "OK, buddy, you give it a try!"

The winged flush, resembling a Fourth of July starburst explosion, was so blindingly startling that the *bang, bang* from my trusty 1948, 16-gauge Model 21 resulted in nothing more than some slightly disturbed, very thin air molecules. I hadn't even resumed breathing yet, when somewhere off to my right, my auditory senses perceived an extremely disconcerting gravelly voice coming from an apparition holding a sweet little John Wilkes 28-gauge located at the very edge of my peripheral vision commenting, "Gotta double—how aboutchoo?" To which I replied with that most scholarly of quotes from the philosopher Homer Simpson by first wincing and then croaking out, "D'oh!"

That same scenario played out a time or two more over the next few days of hunting, but I did finally get the hang of actually stopping the midair flight (mostly on single birds over drop-dead-staunch points) of one or two of the fastest of North America's game birds, the venerable Hungarian partridge. Those little dudes can get outta Dodge in one heck of a hurry.

To this day, almost a decade later, usually when I'm in the middle of nowhere, despite trying to force-focus my concentration on the delicate task at hand, almost every time I approach a pointed covey that gravelly voice still haunts me... "Gotta double!"

PETE'S PLACE
Recollections of a good friend and fine hunts.

The high ground of Pete's ranch was on the sloping side of Sheep Mountain's uplift. The view from the mountain showed the clearly defined borders of his ranch. "I don't believe in having a hired hand," Pete once told me. "The more hands you have, the more cattle you have to raise. Prairie grasslands carry only so many cows and it's much better not to overgraze the land." Which explains why Pete's ranch in Montana was such a haven for upland game birds.

Pete's modest, white single-story house had a traditional front porch shaded by ancient prairie willows. During the warmer months, the porch was a relaxing place to visit with Pete. Once I started talking about the day's events, including the ways the dogs worked, Pete would beam with pride.

One late summer while walking with Pete along the weedy line of a century's worth of old machine parts, my 7-month-old Brittany, Winston, flushed a large covey of Hungarian partridge behind a faded World War II–era Army Jeep. The birds flew toward the cottonwood trees that lined the creek, and I watched them settle in a patch of high grass. Because it was the home covey and never harassed, this seemed like an ideal situation for Pete to watch young Winston attempt to point; I asked if he would like to go with us. "You know, Ben, I would. I've never watched a dog point before," he stated with interest.

Beyond the house, Pete unhooked the metal gate as I studied

the wind direction. After making a large arc below where the covey had landed, I explain to Pete that this big swing would put the dog downwind of the birds. It would give the young pup an abundance of scent, I told Pete.

Winston was twenty feet ahead of us when we approached the grassy area. He slowed, held his head high, and scented the air. I softly told him to whoa as he moved forward hesitantly, and then he stopped. Pete looked at me, and then back at the pup, and smiled. "Good dog," I said. Young Winston took one step and froze, his muscles taut. We watched him for some time before I walked in. By this time, every muscle of Winston's was quivering. "Good dog," I said again, clapping my hands to flush the birds. Winston thundered through the grass, jumped the creek, and chased the Huns up over the hill out of sight.

I allowed a short chase and then called Winston back, but before he returned to me he checked the area where the birds first flushed and he put up a single. Then he was off again, ignoring the whistle. Pete was grinning broadly at seeing young Winston racing around and having the time of his life.

Several days later, through the window, Pete motioned me in with a wave of his hand. He poured a cup of black coffee, and handed it to me. "Would you care to go hunting today?" I asked.

"Can't, have to go to town," he answered.

I knew Pete had no intention of going with me, but after seeing Winston point I just thought he might. He got up from the table and said, "I got something to show you." He turned and walked into the other room. Pete came back into the kitchen with a grin you could see a mile away. "What do you think of this new automatic shotgun I picked up yesterday?" he asked.

He handed me the gun. I put it to my shoulder, looked down the barrel, and handed it back. "Nice, light 20-gauge," I said.

"After seeing that pup of yours, I'd like to try my luck hunting birds with you. But today I got to go to town, forgot to get shells for it," he said a little sheepishly.

I didn't say anything. I had 20-gauge shells in my hunting rig, but there was no need to get them. I knew Pete well enough to know he had no intention of going—though having the shotgun revealed his interest in my activities on his place. As far I know, that shotgun never came out of the box again.

Several years ago, Pete passed away; the ranch sold and passed into good hands. In Pete's will, the total inheritance went to Montana's university system for Montana student scholarships. River Lovec, my grandson, was one of the first recipients of a scholarship as an undergraduate student at Montana State University.

Pete was highly interested in my knowledge of upland game birds, and in the value I placed on his stewardship of land. Being a fine manager of range animals, he also appreciated my ability to train bird dogs. To this day, I have no insight into why Pete chose such an honorable path to help young people further their education through the Montana scholarship program. But Pete was just that way.

After five decades, I'm still fortunate to run my dogs and hunt at Pete's place. His place has always been a treasure—but simply knowing Pete was the real treasure.

MERRI MERRI
River Lovec

There are countless things for which we ought to thank our bird dogs. My own dog, Merri Merri, has taught me a great deal about friendship and trust. She has been my loyal and joyful partner in many adventures and misadventures, and thanks to her theft of a seared, bloody and perfect sirloin off a post-fishing-trip dinner table while the whole party was caught up in big fish stories, I learned a great deal about forgiveness. But I believe I owe her most for the valuable lessons she taught me about love and respect.

I was schooled in the instinctive theory of bird dog training. That is to say, discipline is discipline; but beyond that, let the dog be a dog. Merri Merri was given to me by my grandfather, Ben Williams, when I had just finished high school, and at that time I was beyond excited to have a project more earthly than academic. In many ways, sheer luck made this first dog training experience simpler than I had any right to expect it to be; unlike many Brittanys, discipline came rather naturally to Merri. In fact, if I'm being honest, I must say that she is probably more responsible than I am. Beyond that, I needed only to figure out how to let the dog be a dog.

I reasoned that if she was only to be a dog I needed only to get her outdoors and get out of her way. Luckily I lived in prime bird country and had, as my grandfather and mentor, an exceptionally active bird hunter. For Merri, many days afield were ensured. But I wanted her to be a great bird dog and I wanted to be her partner and companion along the way. By logic that was straightforward if a bit trite, I applied the lessons from my own childhood household: confidence and capability are the result of high doses of love and even higher doses of expectation.

Even when Merri was too young to properly "go afield," I spent every day possible outdoors with her, seeking all the adventures that a retired, sage-bordered hayfield and a shaggy Russian olive windbreak could provide. I smirked but nodded approvingly when she pointed her first meadowlark, indulged her when she flushed and chased her first hare, and scared the wits out of her with a yelling fit when she chased her first deer. Each evening, by the figurative fireside-with-a-glass-of-brandy, I told her very directly and very honestly how much I loved her, how impressed I was by her, and how accomplished I knew she would become. I never expected her to understand English, but I trusted she would understand earnestness.

After going to college I spent more time in seminars than I did the field. During my studies I did the thing that brought me the most heartache but gave Merri the most opportunity to be a bird dog—I entrusted her almost wholly to my grandfather and his patch of land. I spent each weekend that I could spare in the field with them. Each of those Friday nights Merri greeted me by charging towards me down my grandparents' deck, ears perked and tail wagging. It was always like reuniting with an old sweetheart. As her first few seasons passed, my grandfather began remarking that she might be one of the best dogs he'd bred. I quietly took tremendous personal pride in this. Indeed he had bred her. Moreover, he had completed most of her formal training. But I had raised her, so to speak. I respected her enough to let her be a dog, and I loved her enough to help her be her best dog.

UNDER THE BIG SKY
The lure of draft brew can attract unwelcome drop ins.

My friend Pete had a lovely ranch where the foothills gave way to an isolated mountain range underneath Montana's Big Sky. Pete's place was a working ranch, with a modest house. The living room was full of well-worn furniture and had a large, open fireplace. Occasionally we'd sit there, but mostly we visited in the kitchen sitting on chairs made from steel tractor seats.

Pete's house smelled of breakfast, lunch, or supper, depending on when I arrived. If he was in a talkative mood, he offered me something to drink—but never gave me the choice of beverage. He might offer coffee or, after I hunted, wine or beer. I rarely refused because this was his way of asking me to stay longer. If Pete sought more conversation, he gave you a refill before you had a chance to refuse.

I first met Pete in the early 1960s when his land had posted signs that read, HUNTING ON FOOT ONLY, and that's when he gave me permission to park my vehicle in his ranch yard and walk his land from there. By year's end, I had earned his trust and because of his fascination with bird dogs, our friendship blossomed.

I arrived on one trip with my Brittanys, Gina and McGillicuddy, in the backseat of my Bug, a blue Volkswagen of that era. Pete was standing in the opening of a big tool shed as I pulled into the yard. I stepped out of the car, and we shook hands. We kicked a little dirt, talking about the weather. Then I asked if he had seen any Hungarian partridge. Pete thought a while, and then slowly started drawing lines in the dirt with his foot. "The other day, moving heifers off their summer range, I saw several bunches in my high pasture," he said, pointing his finger to the sloping side of Sheep Mountain.

Pointing back to the lines he had drawn in the dirt, Pete continued: "That's four miles from here. Follow the dirt road through three gates and stop by the salt lick. You can drive, so the dogs won't have such a long walk back to the rig when you're done hunting."

That was Pete's way of giving me permission to drive on his expansive ranch property.

I often stopped to see Pete when hunting, even though I had a standing invitation to drive the backroads and walk when and where I liked. I was late one morning, so my plan was to stop later in the day. The light had faded by the time I sat down with Pete. It was Sunday, and the house was thick with heat from the burning logs in the fireplace. I could see in his eyes that he was in a talkative mood.

"Is young Winston with you?" he asked about my Brittany.

"Yes, Pete, he is."

"Bring him in, it's cold outside."

Bringing my dog into his house signaled a longer visit. We sat in the kitchen with Winston at my feet. Same drill. "Ben, would you care for a drink?"

"Thanks, I would."

He got two frosted glasses from the freezer, and then went into the bedroom and came back with the glasses full of cold beer. Up to this time, he had never offered me beer in a glass. After taking several sips, I mentioned that it was very good.

Pete looked at me and said, "It should be, it's draft beer."

I didn't say a word, because with Pete you never asked why. You just waited for him to tell you. I slowly sipped my beer. Pete said, "Aren't you going to ask me about the draft beer?"

"Well, I was, Pete, but I thought better of it."

Pete gave me a half grin and said, "Years ago I built a small, insulated shed against the outside wall of the bedroom to hang meat. I don't use it for that anymore, so I installed a keg of beer and piped it through the wall into the bedroom. That was the closest place to bring it into house."

"Well, Pete, that's a great idea," I said. Fortunately, I was able to escape after my second glass.

A couple of weeks passed before I stopped in to see Pete again. When I finally did, he offered me a drink, which I accepted. This time, it was a can of Bud. I thanked him and took a sip. Pete looked at me for some time, and then started to talk.

"I suppose you would like to know about not having draft beer?"

"No, Pete, this Bud is fine," I said, knowing he'd tell me about it if he wanted to.

It wasn't too long before he began. "Well," he said, "after the second keg went down the gravel road to be delivered here, my closest neighbor, who lives four miles away, figured out it was headed to me. He started coming to see me more often. So I had to put a stop to it."

FIRST FLUSH
Roger Catchpole

I had a William Westley Richards shotgun in my hand, Ben a John Wilkes. An assortment of Brittanys and English pointers stood ahead, motionless.

We approached the point briskly. Ben moved with a gracefulness honed through a lifetime spent chasing Hungarian partridge. I dithered, struggling to read the point. Ben noticed me slowing and urged me forward, beyond the noses of his rock solid companions.

Although I'd rehearsed this moment in my mind, I could feel my muscles tightening with each stride. Racing through my mind were two recurring thoughts: that I'd travelled halfway around the world, and that I hoped I wouldn't blow my chance.

Earlier that day I had landed in Bozeman, Montana, where I met Ben O. Williams, a hunting hero of mine, for the first time. I had journeyed in search of Huns and to learn Hun hunting. And who better to teach me than North America's preeminent Hun authority. Now, three hours later, we were in the field about to shoot our first flush.

It seemed appropriate that I was holding the William Richards, part of Ben's collection of English side-by-side shotguns. I'd lived next to the Westley Richards factory in Birmingham, England, as a student. Clearly, fate had intervened to bring this gun, from the Midlands of England to the High Plains of Montana, for me to shoot.

As I stepped forward a further thought struck me, I was hunting English partridge with an English gun over English pointers (not to forget the Brittanys). All that was missing was England itself. I gave out an audible chuckle.

At that moment a raucous screech pierced the air as a covey of Huns broke cover. Birds rose all around us and made their escape. I raised the 28-gauge to my shoulder and squeezed the trigger, missing an easy crossing bird with my first shot before connecting with my second barrel. Ben watched the scene unfold before smoothly raising his gun and dropping a sleeper.

As the dogs collected our fallen birds Ben congratulated me on harvesting my first North American Hun—even though we both knew I should have made a double.

Following our first hunt, I would return every fall to spend time in the field with Ben and his dogs. Although we shared many points and covey rises in those subsequent years, I will never forget our first flush.

PRIVATE TIME
At certain intervals, some recreational activities are best done alone.

Each new year, my outdoor activities are really new beginnings more than extensions of where I left off the year before. I'm never quite sure if many of my finite learned skills have deserted me between the seasons, so I'm inclined to think certain activities are best done alone. The opening of fishing small streams is one such activity, even though Montana's big rivers are never closed, so I know not all of my angling skills are in remission. However, a small stream takes on a completely different tone than a big river and naturally requires more precise techniques. Tying a 5X tippet to an existing leader and threading it through the eye of a size 16 hook takes different memory and finger dexterity than the big-river setup of an 0X leader tied to a size 2 streamer. Further, when standing in a shrub-lined small trout stream, a high backcast is required, which makes for another complex skill that I'm never quite sure my body has completely retained from one season to the next. So striving to get all of these achievements accomplished, over rising trout, is best done without any onlookers, I feel.

The opening day of hunting season has similarities. I certainly will not be at my best when shooting for the first time in a season, nor will my canine companions be at the top of their games. And because of my antiquity, each year the hills appear steeper, the birds seem to fly faster, and my shooting becomes a little more erratic. So total solitude softens my innate anxieties—I don't want an audience.

Then there is the interval between the hunting and fishing seasons when the fly rods are still and the guns are silent—what I call Gear Time. During this period, being alone is a great pleasure and extends the full year's enjoyment. This is the time during which I sort out every piece of equipment by category, fondle it, admire it, tell stories out loud with physical reenactments of the event described, and test equipment for strength and accuracy—and for the joy of cleaning it.

I do admit to having accumulated an array of fly rods, reels of many sizes, flies tied for world-class streams, shotguns I've kept for nostalgic reasons, shotguns in different gauges for various game birds, plus all the other equipment required for pursuing both highly sophisticated sports—fly fishing and wingshooting.

First out from its aluminum case and silk sleeve is my Medallion Sila-flex Golden, 7½-foot, five-piece fly rod, purchased in 1961. While I'm assembling the rod and attaching the Hardy lightweight fly reel, a high-mountain lake comes into view in my mind's eye. The first cast is next to a large logjam. Slowly I twitch the size 12 grasshopper imitation and out of the depths a large shadow emerges that slowly inhales the fly. The fight is on and after some time, a fat 16-inch westslope cutthroat trout is released back into the crystal blue water. Next out are a couple of old, classy 8- and 10-weight Fenwick rods along with several Pflueger Medalist reels I used when fishing the Florida Keys for tarpon, snook, and bonefish. The Sage and Winston fly rods are uncased and steelhead, Atlantic salmon, sea-run brown trout, and big Alaska rainbows swim though my memory.

Gear Time means taking out my old Lefever 20-gauge shotgun, admiring its age, visualizing a young boy with his dog, and remembering all the ring-necked pheasant missed before one was killed as it flew across the railroad tracks with Mike, my springer spaniel, in hot pursuit. The mental picture changes to a boy and his dog sitting on abandoned railroad tracks admiring the rooster's long, colorful tail. Next, the vintage British double-barreled shotguns are handled with admiration and occasionally shot offseason at clay targets. After cleaning, waxing the highly figured gunstocks, and admiring the fine engraving, each one is put away with loving care.

A few dogs from the kennel also sense when it's Gear Time. Swinging a shotgun pretending to follow a partridge covey has little effect on the dogs' behavior. However, clearing out the hunting vests is quite a different story, for the smell of bird scent and a few old feathers gets their attention. But the high point for getting the dogs excited, with their woofs and cries, is when I drag out my hunting boots from the closet for cleaning and waterproofing. For the dogs, this is a hopeful sign that I may put on a pair, load them up in the hunting rig, and take them for a run.

Gear Time not only takes place indoors, but also in the field. For me, Gear Time outdoors is a private time for training pups and started dogs, or to try out a different shotgun, a new fly rod, or other gear that needs to be worked with and handled. It's a time to wonder about reading a trout stream, to study the flora and fauna, or just to sit on the tailgate of the prairie wagon after a hard day running the dogs and watch the sunset... alone.

ADAM'S WALL
Mike Janeczko

O ne of the reasons that Ben Williams and I hit it off as friends and hunting partners over the years is our similar canine and human hunting philosophies. On the humanoid side our mantra is, walk a lot, laugh a lot, have great fun with the dogs a lot, have a nice post hunt wee dram of scotch and... oh, yeah... somewhere in there somebody actually shoots a bird. I just sum up this philosophy as, "He gets it."

On the furry four-legged side, "Let a dog be a dog" is Ben's canine hunting mantra. By that we don't mean to expect that it is possible to pick up any stray mutt at the pound, turn him loose on opening day and expect him to retrieve like King Buck or point like Elhew Snakefoot.

The process of developing a canine hunting partner of course begins with some careful introspection to first figure out what kind of temperament you have as a hunter, then ascertaining the how, when and conditions of where you mostly hunt. Only then can you follow up with finding a breed of dog with the genetics and disposition that fit your personal situation the best.

Covering miles of terrain quail hunting in the Deep South with a huge pointing black lab that might suffer from heat stroke, or chasing birds through subzero cold in the sloughs of northern Minnesota with a thin-skinned pointer, who might succumb to hyperthermia, might not be the best of choices.

The second phase is imprinting and basic training. Bonding with your new companion and mastering the generic instructions of sit, stay, come and heel takes a lot of time and patience, but will pay big dividends later out in the field.

After graduation from basic training comes the third phase of spending some time in what the military calls the specialty schools. For retrievers its whistle commands, hand signals and things like swimming around decoys to retrieve a feathered prize. For flushers and pointers it's proper range, whoa, steady to shot and all of that stuff. This is the phase that sometimes separates the different training philosophies. This is the phase where "let a dog be a dog" really kicks in. By gosh, those powerful noses, pointing genetics and retrieving instincts have been bred into those critters for about a hundred generations. So let us humans get out of the way and let them do their thing! It is in this phase of development that a control-freak trainer's ego can sometimes ruin what might have been a fine hunting companion.

In that regard, in a brief check of a half-dozen hunting journals, outdoor magazines and dog periodicals, it is apparent that ads for electronic gizmos, collars and beepers of every sort imaginable and GPS's that will track your dog's every move, analyze his brain waves and report back to in real time have become absolutely mind boggling. When did we all become so obsessed with electronics?

But I digress... what I'm attempting to describe here is the next phase. What animal behaviorists refer to as piercing through "Adam's Wall." That is, the very real, yet invisible, unspoken, ephemeral, boundary of perception and communication between man and animal. It is this sort of thing that Jane Goodall mastered with her primate studies.

In my experience, a very few dog men such as the likes of Ben O. Williams (read: Zen Master of the dog world) really get it. The above mechanical training techniques are just temporal window dressing compared to the truly spiritual connection one can make with one's four legged hunting companion. Here I am entering a realm that I can only describe as attempting to describe the indescribable. (Do you hear that Twilight Zone music in the background?) Anecdotally, have you ever experienced a time when out in the field you think to yourself that that little clump of brush over there might hold a bird, only to have your setter/pointer/flusher/retriever jog right over there and promptly flush a covey? Or, more importantly, just the opposite, your bird dog somehow subliminally communicates to you that you indeed are going in the wrong direction and you need to pay attention and follow him/her into the next cover over by this little clump of trees only to have a grouse buzz out, almost taking your hat off?

That is truly the ultimate phase of the hunting experience. Guys like Ben Williams, Gordon MacQuarrie, Gene Hill, Robert Ruark, Jim Harrison, Jose Ortega y Gasset and a few other authors have done a much better job than I have of elucidating how to reach this stage of enlightenment. So next time you're out in the field (preferably just you and your dog), forget the electronics, set your ego aside, let your dog be a dog, and see if you can "get it." Only then will you experience the truly blissful Zen-like joyfulness of crashing through Adam's Wall.

REMEMBERING DAN

Dan Bailey was a master fly fisher and a lover of the outdoors.

At one time, Dan Bailey's Fly Shop in Livingston, Montana, was the most famous fly fishing store in the world. Though the shop was probably best known for its large selection of beautiful, hand-tied flies produced on the premises, and for having a large assortment of finely built bamboo fly rods, it was also headquarters for local anglers and hunters of all ages.

Dan loved fly fishing, but he also loved helping people. He was adamant about selling anglers and hunters what they needed, and only what they needed. He took as much interest in selling a young person the right spinning lure for fishing the Yellowstone River as he did marketing an expensive bamboo fly rod to an expert. Dan Bailey's life and the fly shop that bears his name are legendary in the history of the development of North America's Western trout fishing waters.

Coming from New York, Dan looked westward and chose to set up shop in 1938 in Livingston because he sensed Montana's Missouri River headwaters and the area's mountain streams would remain the best trout waters in the United States. Not long after opening his shop, Dan trained women to tie his in-house flies. Dan always said, "The best production fly tiers are women," and his fly tiers were considered the best in the business. By 1941, Dan Bailey established such an excellent reputation for hand-tied flies that he issued the first store catalog. It featured not only standard patterns but also many of his inventive flies. At that time, these flies were considered the best made.

Over the years, Dan Bailey's Fly Shop proved to be a Mecca for introducing fly fishermen to the area and servicing anglers worldwide with flies. It wasn't long before serious fly fishermen referred to the upper Missouri River complex as Dan Bailey Country.

Being an upland bird hunter and fly fishing enthusiast, I was drawn to Dan Bailey Country for the fishing and also for the untouched upland bird hunting opportunities in the area. In 1962, I sought out and secured a teaching position in Livingston, Montana. Being a high school teacher, I worked several seasons in Dan Bailey's Fly Shop during the summer months when school was out. That's when I got to know Dan personally.

Dan was a conservationist and he suggested we organize a Trout Unlimited chapter. Because he was active in the fly fishing business, he thought it best for me to become the chapter president, but said that he would serve as treasurer. I accepted the challenge and recruited several hard-working local fly fishing colleagues as the other officers.

Within a month Montana's Yellowstone Chapter of Trout Unlimited (TU) was born; it's now called the Joe Brooks TU Chapter. After a year our chapter helped in organizing other Montana Trout Unlimited chapters so we could form the TU State Council. For years, Montana's State Council became the driving force in achieving many important legislative changes that greatly benefited game fish and fishermen.

Upon receiving teaching tenure, I bought several acres outside of town with a small spring creek that supplied water to a large lagoon flowing into the Yellowstone River. I designed and built a single-story house with floor-to-ceiling windows facing the distant Absaroka Mountains and the lovely spring creek. During the seasons, spawning trout, migrating waterfowl, and other fauna frequented the spring creek, creating a wildlife sanctuary.

Dan Bailey and his wife Helen loved the house and its location. When a parcel of land at the end of the lagoon came up for sale, they bought it. Then they asked if I would design a house for them similar to my own, and I did. I sited the Bailey house as close as possible to the lagoon so Dan and his guests could cast flies off the front deck and catch wild trout moving in from the river. Dan's son, John, still lives there today.

I had the opportunity to join in with many of Dan's close friends who were the early fly-fishing pioneers, authors, journalists, and fly-rod lovers coming to fish the Livingston area from all parts of the globe. Lee Wulff, Joe Brooks and Charles F. Waterman, to name a few, are still known today in fly-fishing circles. The names of many other true fly-fishing pioneers from that time have been lost to antiquity.

After I settled in, Thomas McGuane, one of the finest modern novelists of our time, and a friend of mine for many years, and renowned landscape artist/writer Russell Chatham moved to Livingston, and by doing so they inspired others to fish Dan Bailey Country. Norman Maclean (whom I had the pleasure of knowing), author of the highly acclaimed novella (later a well-known movie) *A River Runs Through It*, certainly influenced a new generation of fly fishermen visiting and fishing Dan Bailey's Western waters.

Dan was a good hunter and he liked to hunt. He said his favorite hunting was for mule deer in the mountains.

Not being a trophy hunter, for him it was just a matter of finding any deer, so I would go along to help him if he shot one. We would start in late morning in his International Scout and drive old logging roads glassing for a deer. For some unknown reason, Dan always managed to shoot his deer at dusk, so dragging the animal back to the vehicle was a challenge. Dan was a good woodsman, but there were times he seemed lost while driving; yet we always found a way out. Being with him deer hunting was fun. There were times when Dan and I also hunted ducks and grouse, but he *really* loved to fish.

Together we fished the big rivers, but the quality I remember best about Dan was his love for fishing small outback creeks.

I recall one such place we fished that had an abundance of small brook trout. The clear, coldwater creek was about four feet wide and six feet deep in places, on average, and meandered serpent-like through miles of sagebrush country. One of Dan's special joys was catching trout in places such as this. "In this country," he said, "one can fish for miles and never see another human footprint."

John Bailey returned from college and the Army and joined his father in the business. Following Dan's death, John became the proprietor of Dan Bailey's Fly Shop and has been at the helm ever since. Today, the West has numerous storekeepers with wonderful fly shops, but none will ever equal what Dan and Dan Bailey's Fly Shop achieved in Livingston, Montana. Throughout the years, Dan gave me many treasured memories.

I will always be grateful to Dan for his warm companionship and inspiration. Like Norman Maclean once said, "Dan Bailey was the personification of the sport and a 'master of the art' of fly fishing."

KICKING A LITTLE GRAVEL
Darren Brown

I've shared some wonderful days afield with Ben and his dogs over the years, but one of my favorite times was wandering around with fly rods in the truck instead of shotguns. Ben has always enjoyed showing friends new country, so we drove over the Yellowstone River bridge just down the road, and continued on to where the houses thinned out and then disappeared altogether for long stretches.

It was a gorgeous but stark landscape that was still new to me. We stopped for a bit to watch a family of burrowing owls that Ben liked to check on occasionally as they flitted in and out of gopher holes off an old section road, talked about nearby leks he visited in the spring, and spied plenty of antelope and mule deer along the highway.

Finally reaching a thin ribbon of water well off the angling radar, we stopped to "kick a little gravel" with a rancher who was happy to let us cast a line. Ben has a relaxed, genuine approach to such encounters that opens a lot of doors and often leads to lifelong friendships. It's a style I've tried to emulate through the years with only modest success. Somehow I often appear as if I'm knocking on the door to nervously report running over the family dog in the driveway, rather than to enjoy a friendly visit to inquire about access.

It had been a hot, dry month and the fishing was pleasant but slow, so we marked the place down for future reference and packed up. Just as we were about to relocate, we ran into a friend of Ben's who owned a place down the road. He happened to be on his own way out to fish and kindly led us to a favorite haunt in the mountains, accessed from an improbable spot high above a steep canyon with no water in sight. It grew much cooler as we descended on a faint path, and we eventually broke through the brush to see a beautiful little creek—the kind of water that threads through your dreams if you love solitude more than trophy trout.

We fell into an easy rhythm, leapfrogging from pool to pool, stopping occasionally to watch one another cast to a challenging lie or to play a fish. It felt like a luxury to have so much water to ourselves at the height of summer and we took our time with things. Later we sat for a bit, chatting about wild places and politics and whatever else came to mind, no one relishing the climb back out, but no one complaining. The beer waiting in the cooler felt well earned.

That was many years ago, but it's a day I revisit from time to time as a reminder about how getting away from the famous—and famously crowded—rivers of the West and perhaps kicking a little gravel can lead to a deeper connection to the land and a sporting life rich in friendships as well as good fishing.

A BRIDGE TO BIRDS
Adair Creek intersects the author's longtime hunting tract.

More than half a century ago, hunting Montana grasslands for upland game birds over pointing dogs was unheard of. When I first got permission from my friend Pete to bird hunt on his land, my use of pointing dogs intrigued him. Over the years our friendship grew, and he enjoyed hearing the dog stories, which solidified bird hunting on his place solely for me.

My routine was to drive out from the river valley and turn on the Adair Creek county road, which swings lazily back and forth following the hay meadows along the waterway. But my attention was trained beyond the creek to where the prairie world began. After several miles, the meadow ends and the main gravel road makes a sharp left around a low hill. The entrance to Pete's ranch is straight ahead.

After taking the road that goes to Pete's house, I would carefully cross the worn wooden plank bridge, follow a two-rut trail over the hill, and park in a narrow valley by a wire gate. Across Adair Creek, the rolling hills with the lush riparian draws running through them were the heart of the ranch.

The near side was used for spring and summer grassland pasture, it was land purchased years ago for delinquent taxes after the homesteaders pulled up stakes or went bust. It still has a primeval loveliness about it and you can learn to read the prairie world by tracing its flora and fauna on foot. I'm not going to hide this from you: I never much liked the bridge. It was a hazard to cross. One rainy morning, I finally decided to address the subject of the rickety, unsafe bridge with Pete.

Through the kitchen door window, I could see Pete setting out a pot of hot water for instant coffee, and a box of crackers. He looked up and motioned me in. Across the table, I sat on the red metal tractor seat. Pete moved the pile of newspapers and an *Old Farmer's Almanac* and made a cup of black coffee, sliding it across the table and pointing to the can of condensed milk.

"Thanks, Pete, I'll pass on the cream. How's your day been?" I asked.

"Oh, about the same. Went to town the other day and got a battery for the John Deere 4020. Put it in, got it running, then hooked up the sickle bar. With all this rain the hay meadows are going to have to be cut early."

"Do you think you'll get a second cutting?" I asked.

Looking straight at me, like I should know, he added: "Never do."

After his lengthy conversation covering the *Old Farmer's Almanac* yearly weather forecast, cattle prices being too low and taxes too high, too many folks moving into this county for no good reason, and seeing a new night yard light shining five miles away, I finished my coffee. "More?" Pete asked. Offering more coffee meant he was more interested in conversation than going outside. "How are those young dogs doing?" he asked. Pete loved my dogs, so I reasoned if I included them in the conversation that might entice him into building a new bridge.

"Ran one dog in the hills the other day. Crossed that sagging bridge. Sure hope it lasts this season, so I can work the dogs in the hills. As you know, that is by far the best side to find birds, especially for my young starter pups."

After more dog stories, I suggested doing the labor to build the new bridge and he could use the tractor to place the bridge stringers. Slowly sipping my cold coffee, I was hoping my words sunk in. After a long pause, Pete looked at me, then down at the pile of newspapers, and said, "That bridge is getting old. Looks like it stopped raining, time to get my chores done." End of conversation.

A few weeks from the opening of hunting season, I approached the bridge and to my surprise I saw a neat pile of rough-cut planks and two huge stringer logs. The following Saturday, without inform-ing Pete, I arrived at eight o'clock and started removing the old bridge. It wasn't long before I heard the John Deere tractor start up, and by four o'clock the last rough-cut plank was nailed in place.

One morning after the bird season was well under way, Pete waved me down. He wore a half grin, which meant he had some-thing funny to tell me. Pete said, "The other day I had some guy from town stop by. Never saw him before. Said he heard that you hunted birds on my place and asked if he could go up in the hills. I thought for a while, and then asked him how he planned on getting over there." He pointed toward the new bridge. "'Well' I said, 'Ben Williams built that bridge and he won't let anyone cross it.' And that was the end of that," Pete said, smiling.

FRIEND, MONTANAN AND
RETIREMENT CONSULTANT
Steve Claiborn

Some of my happiest times growing up were at my grandmother's small farm in Missouri. After breakfast I would take off with my .22 Marlin and spend the whole day shooting frogs, tracking small game and generally exploring the Ozarks.

Halfway through my business career I began thinking of the future and concluded that I wanted to retire to the country. During my extensive travels I began researching farm and ranch opportunities and ultimately concluded that Montana was the last best place. After three more years of trying to buy several ranches, one seller hit my bid. I had a hard time finding the ranch when I proudly took my wife and son to see it a couple of weeks later.

Once we found the ranch that first time and performed some basic inspections, I noticed a guy driving around in a pick-up with several dog boxes on top. I asked him what he was doing on "my ranch" and he explained that he was a retired teacher and coach and had been bird hunting on the ranch through several owners for some forty years. He offered to look out after the wildlife in my long absences in return for access to train his dogs and hunt. Buying the ranch at that time was a good deal, but my deal with Ben turned out to be even better.

I had borrowed more money than I could reasonably expect to repay to buy 3,500 acres, 1,700 miles north of our city home in

Texas and I didn't know anything about farming or ranching. But I did want to set myself up for a retirement of the hunting and fishing life.

While I was incredibly lucky with my timing and location, as interest in Montana real estate has rocketed since the early 1990s, I have discovered that the real treasure in Montana is its people. Almost everyone is there because they want to be there.

Ben and his wife, Bobbie, are among the many great folks we have met in Montana, and they are probably Montana's best sales force. Between the two of them, they must have taught half of the long-time residents of Livingston at one time or another. They are both serious naturalists and have built a true nature preserve at their home on the Yellowstone. They love the wildlife that comes calling all year long and the wildlife loves them.

Ben has helped us learn to live in the Northland. The ranch doesn't seem nearly so remote any longer and thanks to Ben's assistance, the hunting is still great and the views unobstructed. He has taught my son and me to hunt and fish in the mountains and has been kind enough to give us three dogs from his kennel. With a little tuning up from Ben, those dogs have to be among the best hunting Brittanys in Montana or Texas. Ben is a great author and photojournalist, and he actually lives the life, successfully.

My plan to retire to the fields and streams is becoming a reality. Nothing is quite so satisfying as the successful execution of a long-term strategy. We have already had three decades of great family adventures at the ranch. Montana has proven to be better than I ever expected, but the best part is the many friends we now have there. Fortunately I expect many more years of hunting and fishing, and a lot of them with Ben. How is it that I have significantly aged over the last twenty-five years and Ben looks the same? I guess if you walk ten miles a day with your dogs you can keep doing it as long as you keep walking.

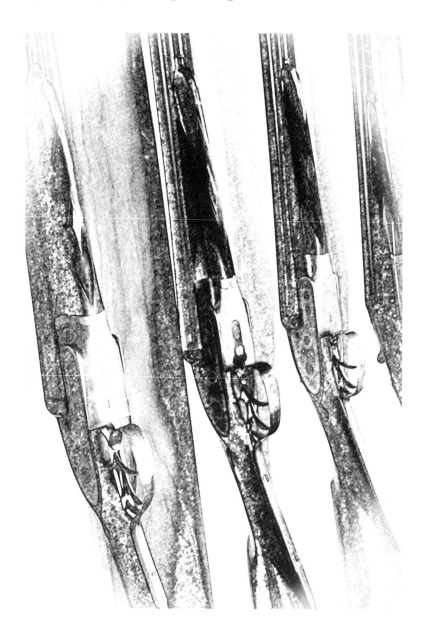

TREASURED OBJECTS
I surround myself with the stuff that has earned a place in my heart.

I grew up on a small farm, and remember with mixed emotions, that after the last snow and the first sign of spring flowers, we had a day called Spring Cleaning. For us kids, it was the opposite of a holiday. With pain and animosity, I witnessed the gathering of my fishing, hunting and camping gear; outdoor books and magazines; flora and insect collections; and other treasures to be scrutinized and put away neatly—or hauled to the dump. Back then, I could never decide for sure if the sentimental value of an item outmatched its usefulness—things such as broken-bladed pocketknives, rusty casting reels, hookless bass plugs, empty shotgun shells, leaky tents, outdated maps and magazines that I cherished back then. I don't know exactly why it was so hard to part with much of that stuff; maybe because it was so hard to get when I was a boy. I can't remember anything I just plain wanted to throw away. Which might explain my large accumulation today of fishing and hunting gear and stockpiles of outdoor books and game-management literature.

It's sometimes embarrassing when a person comes into my study in full view of the hunting and fishing library, yet has no interest in seeing a copy of *Krider's Sporting Anecdotes*, printed in 1853; the complete set of first-edition books by Nash Buckingham; classics such as *Game Management*, *A Sand County Almanac* and *Round River* by Aldo Leopold, the father of wildlife management; a personal signed copy of *A River Runs Through It* by Norman Maclean; a row of Thomas

McGuane and Gene Hill books; and other upland hunting books and biological publications written in the last 150 years.

On my desk, and on the shelf above and hanging on the walls, are many treasured items of memorabilia. For example, my beautiful little Hardy Featherweight reel, which belonged to legendary fly fisherman Joe Brooks and was given to me by Joe's wife Mary after he passed away; it holds sentimental memories of when I fished with him. Or the attractive, smooth, round rock I collected in the pool where I caught my first 25-pound steelhead from the Kispiox River in British Columbia.

I'll admit I'm not surprised when a neophyte seems to be oblivious or uninterested in the book titles or the unfamiliar objects on display; but I'm a little bit surprised that the three beautiful vintage English double guns, showcased in plain view, would not be admired by everyone.

Each one of these lovely, London best sidelock doubles was hand-built between 1880 and 1915, during the Golden Age of British gun-making. The level of quality showcased what the London gun trade was capable of in the Edwardian Era. Each gun has more than 100 years of field-shooting history behind it.

How things have changed. In my younger years, I had several quality shotguns, but admired them only for their function in the field. Largely from reading my historical library, I developed an interest in old British shotguns that began years ago. I care about double guns because they are legendary for their loveliness, lightness, balance and handling when fired.

Let me assure you, I don't show off my British doubles. They have come to me from hard work. But my real purpose for having these fine guns is to share them with my guests when hunting the Montana prairies. In my mind, I'm confident that at one time these English shotguns were traditionally used on the opening day of red grouse shooting in Scotland, when it was mandatory to have a "London Best" 12-bore double to pursue these noble game birds. I feel the same way about the Magnificent First in Montana, the opening day for gray partridge hunting (called Hungarian partridge in North America), a fine European import that deserves the same quality of double gun in the field as its Scottish cousin the red grouse.

When holding one of these lovely English doubles, I have an innate curiosity of the past owners' shooting history. Was the first proud owner shooting driven red grouse with "hot barrels" from lots of time at a butt? Was the next owner shooting high incoming pheasant on a drive? Or maybe the last British owner was rough shooting grouse over flushing dogs during a light Highland rain? All of these—gun, dog and bird—are the roots of my wingshooting passion. On the rare occasion when Huns flush toward me, the vintage double gun in my hand seems so seasoned that it responds as if a past gentleman gunner is doing the shooting for me at driven gray partridge. Every British best gun was made to last forever, and was made to be used extensively in all kinds of weather. My double guns continue adding years to their history, now on the American scene.

My study holds my passions—classic publications, sporting treasures, fine old English doubles, and my pointing dogs resting at my feet.

MONTANA BIRD
Gary Murphy

Eastern Oregon: Gently rolling grasslands at a distance, but up close it was a little more challenging. Steep will wear you out, and after three days of billy goat work, a long drive would be good for the legs.

Kirby Hoyt sells vintage and antique sporting arms as Vintage Doubles and has friends and clients in Livingston, Montana. So we took the gun show on the road, with an invitation to hunt from Ben O. Williams. On leaving the ranch, our host, Steve, asked if I had seen this stretch of country before. I had not. "You're going to want to move."

It snowed the night we got to Livingston. Not much, three to four inches, maybe six in spots. "Disaster," Ben said. "Don't want to break up the coveys in this snow. Too hard on my birds." Hunt postponed. Out of kindness and consolation, Ben and Bobbie fixed us dinner.

There was a little more snow, so we took the next day to meet with Kirby's clients and show best Purdeys, Hollands and fine Scottish and English field guns.

Somewhere on twenty-five years ago I took a different path: French guns—Le Page, Gastinne Renette, Manufrance, Chapu. It was my goal this trip to take my first bird in Montana with a pinfire Fauré Le Page to celebrate the 300th anniversary of that best gunmaker and school to the trade. In business uninterrupted to this day,

Le Page has seen the rise and fall of monarchy, empire, revolution. The French brought us "shooting flying," breech-loading, break-action guns, the cartridge and the centerfire. The British brought us subjugation.

After driving from Oregon in sunny weather and encountering "disaster," we find another consolation. Livingston seems to have a few bars within in walking distance of wherever you happen to be. Weather outside against us; whiskey inside in front of us.

Kirby and I hold up well. Bar 3 was a little more lively, a little more upscale. The bartender was attractive and cheery. Within the line of production on the back bar stood a bottle of Campari. In an effort to impress, I ordered a Boulevardier—Campari, whiskey, vermouth. Very cosmopolitan. She didn't miss a beat: mixed it up, popped in a maraschino cherry, and went back to converse with the regulars. Well, OK, try something else.

"Looking for a fight" is not only metaphoric. If someone is staring at you in a bar, don't stare back unless you want to be asked outside—or on a date. He was a big fella, tweed western-style sport jacket, matching vest, biggest cowboy hat. Even his boots were clean. I noticed this because I really did not want to look up. A calloused, scarred hand the size of Montana spread out on the bar next to me.

"So, what's with the pink drink?"

"Whiskey," I say, "and... ," pointing to the bottle of Campari glowing red. "Makes it bitter. Have a taste."

He took my glass and did. "That's good." He ordered a round of drinks. Seems there was a story here, life change. Had to get out and travel a bit. Sell some cattle. Visit old friends. Out come the photos of his cattle, his front porch, his horse, Music. A lot of pictures of Music. And damn if that horse didn't look like a horse you'd name "Music."

Kirby had been married to a large-animal vet and had seen the insides and outsides of enough cattle. He was soon bored. Our new friend, also bored, headed to the Stockman to see what that was like.

After a couple more bar experiences, we go to bed. Not quite light, there's a call from Ben. Yesterday's sun had knocked the snow off a little and the ground was hard. "Let's go hunting."

There was not much jump in me, but there's no sense wasting happiness. Long underwear for protection, coffee for resuscitation, shotgun shells in anticipation. And guns. French guns.

Ben was loading up his dogs, five or six pointers and Brittanys, as we arrived. Kirby has Brittanys, so he goes all mushy—baby talk and lovey-dovey—as he helps Ben get the dogs up the ramp.

Not far out of town, we are through a gate and on a farm two-track. The ground may be hard, but with grass on top there's some sideways sliding as we climb. Soon I see why Ben didn't want to get stuck out here. Big Sky Country. Isn't the sky the same size every-where? The beginner's mind, the empty eye, puts landscape into con-text. The sky is the same; the bowl is bigger. The bezel around the lens. On top of a plateau, mountains and sharp low hills surround, and I can see what makes vast, "vast."

Now if we were hunting in Michigan, I'd say the dogs had just run off. But if the country's big, the dogs run big. What Ben has figured out is that it's not how far they go, it's what they do when they get there.

The snow interrupted by stones, grass clumps, and bare patches makes the dogs hard to see. But dogs move, and in concert they come to point surrounding a covey. "Let's walk," Ben said, and we cover three to four hundred yards. The dogs moved up. "Keep going. The dogs will stop when we get in shooting range." The dogs held. "Walk in on them..."

There was a burst of fifty or so birds going hard away. One Hun, however, came toward me, the sun highlighting perfect painterly forms and color. Then it recognized "human" and turned a soft right to left. No wingshooter would ask for more. That's when my self-awareness kicked in. I had not moved. Slack and silent, my gun crooked in my arm. Disaster.

I turned to face Ben and Kirby, who were trying to choke some of the hurt out of their belly laughs.

That could have ended our day. The ground was getting greasier, but we moved on to give me another chance. The play of dogs and birds worked out about the same. A going-away shot and I took my first bird in Montana. Grilled it in Oregon, back at the ranch, where Steve asked, "How'd you like Montana?"

I want to move.

HUNS IN SEPTEMBER
The joys of the Montana's Magnificent (September) First.

This says it all about the start of hunting season in my area of Montana: "Hunting Hungarian partridge is one of the greatest cardiovascular programs there is. Huns are also one of the most difficult birds a dog will ever be asked to handle." So wrote Thomas McGuane in the preface to my book *Huns and Hun Hunting: The History, Habits, Habitat, and Techniques of Hunting a Great Game Bird*, published by Willow Creek Press. Now that we're nearing September, I'm pleased to have spent so much time working my bird dogs this past summer. I feel a lot less guilty about all the dead branches scattered under the cottonwoods in the yard and other chores calling for attention as I drive off to train the four teenage canines and to work the older dogs.

Coming soon is the Magnificent First, the Opening Day of Hungarian partridge (also called Huns or gray partridge) hunting season in Montana. I feel a hunter can be excused for being distracted from the endless chores that seem to pile up toward the end of summer. During this time, I not only had dogs to run, but also had other important activities, such as walking miles to scout out the high-plains terrain in search of Hun covey hangouts before the season gets started.

The experienced dogs know the calendar as well by the autumnal smells. Even though the adolescent Brittany sisters and the two English pointer youngsters lack fall hunting experience, they too sense the older canines' enthusiasm and feel something exciting is about to happen.

If I had to choose one game bird to hunt, it would be Hungarian partridge. It's not only the hunting of Huns or having a handful of feathers that first created the appeal that later grew into a passion; what attracted me was the challenge of acquiring biological knowledge to help in pursuing a little-known non-native game bird in North America using gun dogs. It involved a game bird that demanded physical endurance, cunning dog work, and a feeling as wild as the big open county in which they live.

For me, Huns are a creation that justifies having a kennel of gun dogs year-round and to have the opportunity for several months to shoot a few grays for the edification of the dogs and the glory of the table.

I'm sort of bent in the direction of calling my two pointing breeds "gun dogs." That phrase accurately emphasizes a canine's ability to hold a game bird at great distances and to further ensure the gunner will actually be ready to shoot over the dogs. I'd love to have five bucks for every time I've walked up behind one or more of my gun dogs on point a quarter mile away, gun ready, and have a covey of Hungarian partridge flush in my face.

I sometimes wonder if I would be as enthusiastic hunting Huns over gun dogs without having added a few good shotguns to the mix. By "good," I mean older, classic English double side-by-sides steeped in wingshooting tradition. I don't shoot any better with such guns, but they give me a great deal of pleasure having such loveliness in hand, hunting an English game bird (as Huns are), and adding a bit to the history of the English game guns.

There may not be a perfect Hun gun. In fact, I have guns for different times of the day. The morning gun is often one of my 12-gauge London Best side-by-sides, while my afternoon gun is a sleek little 28-gauge side-by-side made in Birmingham, England. At my age, I get a bit tired walking for several hours in the morning, so later in the day the light (five pounds) side-by-side comes up a bit faster than the 12-gauge guns.

If I could design a perfect Hun hunting season in Montana, it would look like this: I'd shift the first two weeks of September to the end of the month, after the frost had bitten the forbs and strangled the fresh green aroma, so the dogs smelled only the fragrance of bird scent. I'd leave October the way it is, but steal the same nice fall weather for November and December right up to New Year's Day, when the bird season closes. That would give me four months of good dog scenting conditions and uninterrupted, pleasant hunting weather.

My memory has a habit of exaggerating the reality, but my true pleasure has always been walking with my gun dogs, having a graceful, lovely English double gun in my hand during beautiful weather, while hunting wonderful game birds. As I write this, I'm thinking about the Magnificent First, and of loading up the gun dogs in the hunting rig, taking a couple English guns, hunting for several hours, and not caring all that much about shooting a Hun.

For me, that's pretty much how it ought to be.

THE UTAH CONNECTION
Jason D. Robinson

"The dogs can find four coveys between us and the ridge over there, you know in a good year." Ben is always pointing and thoroughly explaining things as we bounce down the two-track dirt road in his worn but well-maintained truck and iconic dog boxes. His teaching background is evident as he takes time to make sure I understand the point he is trying to make. Being a bird hunter and biologist from Utah I could imagine there being four coveys between us and the ridge over there. However, Ben was talking about the ridge four hundred yards away; I was looking at the mountain ridge a mile away. I had never seen bird numbers like that. But it is simple: great habitat produces birds.

I am a book worm, have been since a child. Combine a love of reading with a love of bird hunting, and it was inevitable that I would start to read books written by Ben O. Williams. His books inspired me to become an upland game biologist, and to have a kennel full of Brittanys (a good game bird biologist needs great bird dogs). Ben's books led me to eventually write a letter asking if I could travel up to Livingston, Montana. I wanted to learn more about Huns and sharp-tailed grouse, and who better than Ben? A few days later I received a call. Ben offered to let me come look at habitat with him. I was beyond excited. I was going to have the opportunity to learn from the best.

I made the long drive to Livingston the next spring. Most biologists know that a few months in the spring is the bottleneck of upland game populations, those few critical months determine how many birds will be around in the fall. Therefore it is the time of year we focus on habitat. I have devoted my life to understanding game birds, and you don't have game birds without good habitat. Habitat is the key. It determines everything.

We drove from site to site looking at spectacular country and saw ideal habitat for Huns and sharpies. The big rolling prairies with sagebrush hills and deep riparian corridors made ideal habitat for the birds. I was also able to watch his legendary Brittanys work their magic. You can learn a lot by watching and listening to true wisdom.

We spent two full days looking at and talking about habitat, bird behavior and dogs. I absorbed all I could. I wanted to take this knowledge home and grow more Huns and sharp-tailed grouse through habitat work. Will Utah ever have the ideal habitat like Livingston? Probably not, I don't control the weather. However we can make slight adjustments to the landscape to create more habitat, which in turn results in more birds. And isn't that the one thing all bird hunters can agree on—more birds is a good thing!

THE REASONS I HUNT
Game birds, gun dogs and bird guns are the
trifecta that keep me hunting.

Dogs, game birds and fine shotguns are fixed in the forefront of my thinking, and therefore I've always believed that hunting is paramount to a daily work schedule. As a teenager, I had a limited desire for work—I did enough to earn money to buy a shotgun so I could take my untrained springer spaniel on a real bird hunt. I marked each day on the calendar and calculated the number of newspapers to be delivered after school before I had enough money to buy the shotgun and a box of shells. Don't get me wrong: I've always had a high regard for a good work ethic, but I learned early in life that while work feeds one's outdoor ambitions, it also restricts long periods of continuous sporting endeavors unless both—working and hunting—are available in the same neighborhood.

As I got into adulthood, I chose a couple of professions that played a role in allowing me more time afield, without jeopardizing my work principles. For me, the secret was having a place to play just beyond the doors of where I worked. Back then, finding a job that fit my criteria, and paid a living wage, was a real challenge. Teaching worked for me.

I picked the prairie as my place to be a bird hunter. Not because it was a highly cardiovascular program to extend a masculine image, but because of a personal devotion to what my canines were bred to do, to carry on a lovely art form, and to occasionally shoot an incredible iconic fast game bird, the Hungarian partridge. Today, I hunt to surround myself with big-running bird dogs in an open wilderness prairie world where magnificent prairie game birds live, and to spend time in this splendid landscape.

I'm afraid that if I had not chosen to come West when I did, and instead had taken a job in a large city, or become wealthy (just as all of us have wished from time to time), I would have missed a lot of fun from my lifelong hunting experiences. If I hadn't moved to Montana, I doubt I would have really appreciated walking for untold miles across the open prairie in search of a game bird that local folks said could not be hunted. I'm speaking of Hungarian partridge, of course. To hunt this way, I've worn out more shoe leather than it takes to make a Western saddle. After trudging across miles of open prairie, shooting one or two Huns has always made the hunting experience considerably more valuable, the same way that as a kid ice fishing was always more fun if you skipped school to do it.

More than fifty years ago, when I first started hunting in Montana for Hungarian partridge using gun dogs, this was a fairly exotic activity in a country dominated by big-game hunters. Huns clearly are among the most difficult birds a dog will ever be asked to handle. So this exotic, nonnative bird became a real challenge, and may have been the sole reason I became so devoted to a crusade to prove Hungarian partridge could be hunted successfully with pointing dogs.

I must say, it took quite some time to achieve this proof and I needed a completely different training approach to understand my dogs' instincts. The right method was to let a "dog be a dog," to allow it to work a long way off, but still be under my control, which required a soft hand and no whistle.

Each one of us honors our hunts in his own way, knowing that these experiences enrich our life. To become a competent hunter requires a lot more than just carrying a gun afield. A true hunter develops a complex set of learned skills and follows a code of hunting ethics, respecting the quarry, learning their habits and habitat, and having a sense of how the birds use their surroundings. A true hunter has to memorize the geography, be comfortable in different kinds of weather, and understand the limitations of his dogs and gun. One has to learn to walk a little slower to appreciate a sense of belonging to the prairie landscape.

Go afield often enough, and stay long enough, and you will no longer be a stranger to the micro-world around you. If you work diligently and often at these aspects, you will become a better hunter and you also become a part of the place you hunt.

A few of my hunting friends have asked, "Why didn't you trophy hunt for big game… or field trial dogs… or trap shoot… or do some other Montana outdoors activity with real excitement?" My answer is always the same: My challenges are more personal, more tranquil, and my goals more environmentally satisfying. I go to escape the competitive world and not to perform in it. The way I hunt the Big Sky prairie for game birds—over gun dogs with bird guns—is tied directly to the reasons I hunt.

THE COACH
Dan Martin

I started upland hunting a little late in life, at the age of fifty, right after the millennium in 2000. I considered myself very fortunate in that my wife's sister and her husband own a beautiful ranch in Montana. This is truly a sportsman's paradise with healthy herds of elk, mule deer, antelope and upland game birds. Most of the birds are Hungarian partridge and sharp-tailed grouse. I quickly fell in love with Montana and wanted to immerse myself in what I consider a healthy lifestyle. I wanted to be an upland bird hunter.

I first met Ben Williams at a dinner party at the in-laws ranch in 2001 and talked with him for two hours, listening to his story. We are both originally from Illinois, which made his life journey even more intriguing to me. We talked about Ben's life in Montana, his bird dogs, and his philosophy of hunting and training. Also, during the course of that conversation, Ben told me that he had taught school and coached high school football and basketball. He reminded me of a wrestling and football coach that I'd had in high school, a person that I had looked up to and admired, someone that you did not want to disappoint.

The following year, I flew out to Montana to spend four days upland hunting with Ben and my brother-in-law, Steve. It was a great experience and included a lot of excitement, and over the years we have had many enjoyable hunts together. Since that time, I have greatly enjoyed my friendship with Ben Williams. Whether just running his dogs in the field without shotguns, or watching them work birds during hunting season, a beautiful point is always a pleasure. Beyond just hunting and dogs, Ben is a good guy to talk to about life in general. After a day in the field, sitting over a glass of Famous Grouse and solving the problems of the world with Ben is a pleasant ending to a satisfying day.

Two years ago Ben gave me a Brittany puppy from one of his litters. Angus has been a great companion and an awesome upland bird dog. I consider Ben a great friend and coach.

PLEASANT PHEASANT
Hard but pleasant work often makes for a more satisfying hunt.

Years ago, I spent some time hunting pheasant. Back then in Montana, you could hunt anywhere—it was just a matter of getting in your rig and going. Pheasant didn't top my list of favorite game birds, but I went because my hunting partner loved to shoot roosters.

We'd swap weekends driving our look-alike Volkswagen Beetles in pursuit of pheasant-hunting haunts. At that stage in our lives, driving in bad weather on awful roads never bothered us. In fact, we looked upon severe weather conditions as the best time to hunt pheasant.

I supplied the dogs, and he brought the lunches. Gasoline was reasonable, mom-and-pop motels were cheap, and cafés with checkered oilcloth table settings were part of the experience. We viewed these trips not as recreational retreats, but as hardcore hunting adventures.

During one trip, it was so cold the Volkswagen defroster didn't completely clear the frost off the windshield. A foot of new snow was on the ground and the temperature was below zero. I parked the car and we stepped out into the crystal-clear cold. The two Brittanys didn't mind the temperature. They were pacing back and forth, kicking up powdered snow, encouraging us to hurry. Hoarfrost covered the dogs' eyelids and muzzles by the time we got going. I slid down the incline, gaining speed until the cattails stopped my fall at the edge of the long slough. The two dogs never hesitated crossing the cattails and were out of sight before I regained my footing. My next step was worse. A covering of snow concealed thin ice, which broke beneath both feet. Icy water leaked over the tops of my insulated pac boots, instantly freezing my canvas trousers. My partner was slowly plowing through the cattails farther down the slough, apparently walking on hard-frozen ice, waving me on, as a flock of pheasant piled out the far end of the cattails with the two Brittanys in hot pursuit.

"I hate pheasant and where they live," I announced, and headed for the Volkswagen.

After some time, the Volkswagen's floor heater started to put out warm, flowing air. I partly dried my boots and thawed out the bottoms of my trousers. Trying to put socks and pac boots on under wet hunting pants while sitting in the front seat of Volkswagen Bug is like trying to get coveralls on in the back of a Super Cub airplane. It can't be done efficiently. So I hung out the front door of the Bug, pulled on a dry wool sock over a cold wet foot, and then laced up the boot. This accomplished, I stood and did a single-foot balancing act, getting on the other sock and boot.

Shortly after my sock hop, my hunting partner returned. "What are you doing back at the hunting rig?" he said with a half grin, the two happy Brittanys jumping up and down. "Did you see all the roosters blow out the end of the cattails?" he asked, and laughed. "Both dogs pointed rock solid, but the birds didn't hold. There must have been fifty of them. Let's go get 'em!"

We headed in the direction where he had first crossed the frozen cattail slough. He and the dogs were in high spirits, leading the charge to where the pheasant went. After a hard day's hunt, my feet were still wet, but warm. We both managed to kill a couple roosters, still short of our limit. Halfway to the motel, the Volkswagen heater warmed us up, and the cold-nosed and exhausted dogs were curled up on the backseat.

Several years later, I happened to be in that same area. It was early afternoon, and I stopped to hunt about the same time of year. I parked my full-size pickup over the lost tracks of the Volkswagen. I put down three dogs, a pointer and two Brittanys, and slowly angled down the incline. It was shirtsleeves weather and much too warm for pheasant hunting. The slough no longer carried spring-fed water. Smooth brome grass had replaced most of the cattails, except at the far end, where the cattails were clustered in a small triangular patch, 30 feet by 30 feet.

All three dogs froze at the edge of the cattails. The young pointer broke first, followed by the Brittanys. The cattails vibrated as the dogs plowed through the heavy cover, sending bursts of catkins aloft. It was over in seconds. Two single roosters flushed moments apart and I put both of them down. I slowly removed the two empty hulls from the 16-gauge side-by-side, and watched five other big roosters feather the wind and sail toward the river breaks. Two birds were enough, so I headed for the hunting rig. Driving out, I remembered the past hunt in zero-degree weather, the numbers of pheasant lifting out from the slough, me laughing while I did the sock hop, having fun chasing pheasant up and down the breaks in cold feet, the cramped hunting VW, and two happy and hardworking bird dogs curled up on the backseat. The two pheasant on my return trip were too easy. One thing I've learned over the years—hard work makes for a better hunt.

HOMEPLACE
Steven Dodd Hughes

Ben Williams is the reason I have lived in Livingston, Montana since 1995.

I came to Bozeman to visit my good friend Tim, looking for a small town in which to relocate my workshop and my life. Tim had set up a lunch so I could meet Steve Bodio who was living there at the time. I had been corresponding with Steve for a number of years and while we were at lunch in walked Ben Williams and another fellow.

I knew of Ben's writing and photography and it was a pleasure to meet all this magazine talent in the same place. Ben asked, "What are you doing in the area?" and I replied, "Looking for a place to live." Ben, "Livingston's a nice town, if you can handle the wind."

I found my dream-come-true workshop and bungalow in Livingston the next day, and it has been my homeplace for 22 years since that first meeting.

Of course Ben invited me bird hunting, but we didn't get that together for several years. In the meantime, I would run into Ben at the Post Office in the morning. He would keep me informed on the outlook for the upcoming bird season and we would talk about photography, guns, magazines, editors, what stories we were working on and trade talk.

Years went by and Ben found out that my hobby was bird watching. Ben's hobby is paying attention to all things natural going on around him. He is particularly in tune with his own small acreage, where he built his home, workshop and kennels. It is a bit more than a stone's throw from the Yellowstone River, and in this country the actual riparian areas are relatively small. Ben's home is located near the site of the original homestead that was there before the land was subdivided. He had an early pick and chose the grove of ancient cottonwood trees that now surround his workshop/kennel and one side of his home.

Ben is the only guy I know that planted sagebrush as a yard ornamental—lots of sagebrush. He piles the brush and limbs from the scores of trees that he planted and watered so the rabbits and birds have ground cover. I've ridden around his place on a tractor listening to Ben tell the thoughts behind his planting and how he has cared for them over the years.

But my favorite Ben Williams' story has to do with an early morning breakfast at his home. Ben's lovely wife Bobbie fixed pancakes while we watched the birds at the feeder in front of his large glass window. We heard a distant chortling as a pair of sandhill cranes came closer and landed in Ben's front yard to feed on the corn he had left for them.

While I was at Ben and Bobbie's home I found out a lot more about our shared interests: ancient shards from a Pueblo pot they had gathered on a trip to the Southwest decades ago, along with baskets and weavings, and my all-time-envied living room ornament, a whale vertebrae picked up in Alaska long ago.

Sure, I've talked double guns with Ben and had the privilege of writing a story about him and his preferences for 28-gauge doubles for hunting gray partridge. I've been bird hunting with Ben and his Brittanys and English pointers, watching the dogs cross canyons and ridges looking for birds before we really left the truck. I will never forget how he pointed out the geology of our homeplace from high on a hilltop—all of the upthrusts like Sheep Mountain are facing the same direction.

This is our homeplace and Ben has enlightened me to its nuances with many of our Post Office chats and time in the field. He found this place many decades ago by way of an advertisement for a teaching position. I found it more recently, thanks a bit of serendipity and Ben's suggestion. Moving to Livingston was the best decision of my adult life, but Ben's warning was no joke! Take it very seriously, because the wind has almost driven me out as it has many others, though I suspect that Ben and I are here for the duration.

Thanks, Ben.

TOM, ABBEY, AND ME

Born with a hunting heart, Abbey was allowed to fulfill her desires.

Mist rose above the size 16 Light Cahill dry fly drifting lazily with the current along the grassy bank. I was alone, fly fishing on a midmorning Sunday in June in the 1960s, and the only sound was the slow rush of water around my Hodgman waders. The dry fly disappeared, the water erupted, and a trout catapulted two feet in the air, causing the fly line to zing through my fingers. Soon, I brought the fish to hand. After releasing the big brown trout, I noticed an unfamiliar vehicle parked next to mine. Apparently, I had an audience watching the action.

This was an ideal place for two young sportsmen to meet for the first time. The stream is now famous: Montana's Armstrong Spring Creek. At that time, Thomas McGuane was writing his first book, *The Sporting Club*, and I was working that summer at the renowned Dan Bailey's Fly Shop in Livingston. Though going in different directions, we stayed in contact over the years about the wonderful aspects of Montana's outdoor sporting life.

Fast forward a couple decades. Several years ago, my good friend Tom, now known as the author of many fine books, handed me a paperback edition of a collection of nonfiction essays called *Some Horses*, released in 2000 by a major New York publishing house.

After reading Tom's delightful book, which certainly conveyed his knowledge of training cutting horses, it was apparent that our approach to training working animals was similar. My training philosophy is to "let the dog be a dog"—not training them on a string, and letting the game bird scent wake up their genetic instincts so they can perform what they were bred and born to do. What I have learned over many years of raising and training dogs is that dogs think in a logical way, yet nothing like we do. Their logic is much simpler than ours, and most of a dog's brain is used for sensory perception.

A pointing dog with good sensory genes cannot be hurried or forced into learning to use its nose. It has to come naturally, on their terms. For a canine to achieve this, the hunter has to get out of the way, letting the dog be on its own and allowing wild birds to train the dog. The more opportunities a dog has in the field hunting wild birds, the more knowledge and experiences it gains. Dogs are also attuned to subtle changes in temperature, humidity (or dryness), and barometric pressure that we humans cannot detect. These subtleties also have to be experienced and learned out on the landscape. The more opportunities a dog has to go afield, the more a dog learns to decipher and mentally store different weather and other conditions for future application.

I learned that Tom McGuane's philosophy for developing cutting horses is much the same as mine is with dogs. Simply put, Tom writes, "Timing is everything! You have to have a sense of timing to let the horse's own timing rise to the fore. This is known as 'getting out of the way' or, more to the point, 'letting the cow train the horse.'"

For as long as I've known Tom, he has owned a pointing dog of one breed or another. At one time, Tom had a fine Gordon setter, but age and miles of hunting take their toll on any hardworking bird dog. Back then, he gave me a call long before bird season and picked my brain about dogs getting old, us getting older, fishing places, hunting covers, and maybe getting a started pointer pup. I mentioned that I was working with two Brittany pups and a couple of young pointers, along with my kennel of trained bird dogs.

I explained that all four young dogs were coming along, but they needed as much time as possible in the field when the hunting season started. What I did next was a bit unorthodox, but knowing Tom's ability and enthusiasm with dogs and how he hunts wild birds, I suggested he use one of my young pointers for the season.

I learned that Tom not only has the gift of alliance between humans and horses, but he also has the same connection with hunting dogs. In my heart, I knew my young pointer Abbey would be hunted often. Sure enough, before the Western hunting season came to a close, Abbey became a highly qualified bird dog. Then Tom took her south to hunt wild bobwhites. She was his hunting companion, his fly fishing buddy on the bonefish flats, and a cuddly house pet.

Do I have any regrets about giving Abbey to Tom? Not in the least! She couldn't have had a better hunting life, and for her that's just how it should have been.

GOOD FRIENDS
Tom Petrie

It requires dedicated decades of travel and experience to become a world-class angler and bird hunter like Ben O. Williams. As those decades rolled on and his skill sets increased, so too did his age. Yes, Ben has become, ahem, an "elderly gentleman," but one with incredible vitality and enthusiasm.

Example: After two days of humping the High Plains of Montana behind Ben's renowned string of dogs pursuing prairie birds, I confessed that I was played out. Mind you, Ben has roughly twenty years on me, yet he didn't show the slightest fatigue from our ramblings.

"Maybe we'll go fishing tomorrow so you can rest up," he said.

So it was that on day three we were crossing the shallow, tail end of a rapids on the Oxbow. At Ben's request we were hand in hand as an aid for balance.

"This doesn't get any easier these days, does it?" I said over the sound of the rushing water.

"At least we're out here," he said, head down, picking his way slowly across the rocks. "Not everyone can say that."

Reaching the ankle-deep water along the opposite bank, Ben suddenly jerked his hand from my grasp.

"Let go of me!" he shouted in mock indignation. "I don't need your help!"

We shared a laugh then separated, Ben walking to the head

of the rapids we had just crossed while I moved downstream and around a bend to fish a deep run with an inviting undercut bank. Tall, dense meadow grass separated us from sight, yet we were in distant voice range. I had just missed a strike while nymphing through the top of the run when I heard an excited, high-pitched holler, "Tom, Tom, help!"

I dropped my fly rod and ran in the direction of the startling shout. Terrifying possibilities raced through my mind as I struggled through the meadow grass. Has he fallen into the rapids? Mired himself? Heart attack? As I broke into the open there was Ben standing at the edge of the rapids with his rod bent at an extreme angle. My eyes followed the rod tip down the fly line to the leader to the crayfish fly, which was hooked fast to a tremendous rainbow. He glanced at me quickly before returning his attention to the fish.

"Tom, help. No net. I can't get him up the bank myself."

It measured out a tad over twenty-five inches before its release.

As I extended my wet hand in congratulations he said playfully, "Not bad for an old man, if I say so myself!"

Agreed, Ben, not bad at all.

FISHING THE OXBOW
Rising trout, like rising game birds, are locked in my memory.

The sun was just up over the hills by the time I got there. The grass was still wet when I parked the vehicle on high ground above the meadow. There was the oxbow with its sparkling, silver, clear water wrapped around a hundred acres of green meadow. As I was walking the meadow toward the river, water droplets collected on my trousers and wet my sneakers. I stopped just short of the stream's edge, so as not to disturb any fish. Upstream, where the oxbow curved toward me, a brushy logjam on the far side was creating a deep channel under an overhanging bank and a sandbar on the near side.

I studied the long, deep run for even the slightest movement on the surface of the water. It has always a good place for big trout to hang out, including one warm spring morning much like this one when I caught my biggest brown trout in the oxbow. He was a big-jawed male, but rather slim for his length. After a long fight, I moved the heavy fish into shallow water. Holding the fly rod in my left hand, I lowered it just above him. He measured about twenty-seven inches. With my other hand deep in the cold water, I released the trout from the barbless hook and guessed his weight at over four pounds. But that was then. This is now.

A muskrat slid down the far bank in the spot where I'd hooked the big trout, his wake widening as he exited the water on the near side and scurried across the sandbar. Something on the surface of the water caught the sun. My heart tightened as a large bulge on the silvery surface began chasing after the wake. I felt that old feeling of catching that big brown again and carefully scanned for more movement on the water. After some time a kingfisher crossed over the stream, its shadow interrupting my search.

The sun had covered the meadow by the time I crossed over to the opposite side of the oxbow. There the water appeared low, extending the gravel bar farther out into the river. Opposite the gravel bar, a vertical rocky outcropping squeezed the water flow into a fast chute, creating riffles before it trailed off into a long deep run. Downstream, several rising trout caught my eye. I watched them for a long time with their noses in the current taking something off the water.

Streamside, a willow branch wet my hands catching a willow stonefly. On the gravel bar at water's edge, I pitched him into the fast-moving current. He floated rapidly down the chute into the long, flat pool. In a quick circle that broke the smooth surface of the water, the insect disappeared. A trout had taken it.

Fishing for wild trout is similar to hunting prairie grouse and gray partridge. Both take biological knowledge of the quarry, awareness of the ambient conditions, and persistence to fulfill a day's memory.

Sometimes, I methodically use small dry flies or nymphs all day to fish the oxbow. But other times I use a large streamer pattern, fish only the deep runs for big trout, and pass through rather quickly to cover more water. Both methods work, depending on the stream flow, activity of the aquatic life, and fish movement. So what works one day does not necessarily work another day.

From the headwaters to its confluence, the river adds water

volume along its great distance. The part I fish meanders through a long, flat, narrow meadow—once a large shallow lake during the Pleistocene epoch—where the river is more like an isolated stream, little known to most folks, that can be waded using hip boots most of the year.

Back at the vehicle, I felt happy taking the fly rod out of the aluminum case, joining the four sections together, locking the reel on the rod, and threading the forward-tapered floating fly line through the guides. My excitement continued as I put on hip boots over heavy dry socks and then secured all the other paraphernalia in my fishing vest.

I was confident the 6-weight rod would work well for any situation the river had to offer. Stepping into the stream, I dropped a thermometer in the water and waited for the results. The water temperature plus the day's weather suggested that the fish would be active.

From my fishing vest pocket, I removed and opened a large a box of assorted flies, tied especially for the oxbow. Visualizing the big bulge in the water that followed the muskrat's wake and the fish rising in the long deep run, I said to myself, selecting a fly, "When fishing the oxbow, it's all perception."

THE ONE THAT GOT AWAY
Jeremy Petrie

I should preface this story with the fact that I'm a fairly novice fly fisherman. After parking the pickup on a small knoll overlooking the river, we donned our waders and jointed our rods. Ben pointed to a sharp bend in the river and recalled stories of the big trout he'd pulled out of there over the years. I was surprised, excited and touched by his selflessness when he insisted that I fish it. I was as confident that a big fish was holding there as I am when Ben says in the field, "There should be birds over there," and sure enough, a covey rises. He led me upstream of the bend and explained in detail the specific technique for fishing it from the bank. Ben then walked farther upstream and out of sight to cover another part of the river.

It was on the third cast, as my fly dropped deep in the hole, that I felt a hit like never before on a fly rod. The trout rushed from beneath the undercut into shallow, fast-moving water where I caught sight of it. This was a big fish. When he hunkered back under the bank I was able to catch my breath and return to a somewhat regular heartbeat. As he took off again downstream I was ready to call Ben for a net, then remembered that neither of us was carrying one. I was able to turn the huge trout and get him closer but feared that my rod, or the leader, would break at any second.

I thought, this is it, if I have any chance to land this monster I'll have to go in after him. Without thinking twice I jumped in. Soon I had him right in front of me and decided he had to be thirty inches long. I raised my rod high overhead with my right hand while struggling in vain to cup him under the belly with my left. I repeated this clumsy effort three times before the fly slipped from his kype jaw and he disappeared. I trudged to the shallows and dropped to my knees in defeat. I must have stayed there five minutes going over what had just happened, heart still racing.

After gathering myself, I walked a short way back upstream where I found Ben. His face lit up with genuine joy as I tried to put what I had experienced into words (and, he tells me, rather animated hand gestures referencing the size of the fish). He actually enjoyed my having had the experience and the chance to share the story more than he'd have liked to catch that fish himself.

I'm not sure if he chuckled harder when I told him I thought that trout was thirty inches, or when I swore I'd bring a net next time.

BILL'S PLACE

Willow Creek is connected in my mind to a wonderful rancher friend.

The two middle letters of the name on the mailbox are gone, the farmhouse and outbuildings look rather unused, but fresh tire tracks beneath the pickup parked next to the house tell me Bill's around. I knock on the front door. Through the window a dangling single light bulb illuminates the kitchen, but nothing moves. I knock again, then hear the scuffle of feet. Finally, the doorknob turns slowly, and a small, bent man in bib overalls with a weak smile and a soft voice says, "Hellooo, Ben. Come in," he says softly, and then turns and I follow him to the kitchen.

Over the years, his place became a treasure for me to hunt with its overgrown brushy boundaries, meandering creek, uncut corners, and nonharvested crops. Sounds like bad farming, but Bill didn't look at it that way.

Bill was born in a sod-roofed log cabin that his father chiseled by hand through sheer determination and stubbornness. He grew into a small-grained boy—wiry, hardworking and independent—with an older brother and two younger sisters. He quit school on the last Saturday before his 12th birthday when, cooking a jackrabbit with a friend on an open fire in the attic, the pair burned the country schoolhouse down. Before the flames engulfed the rafters, Bill and the neighbor kid lit out across the sage hills like two scared coyotes. His two sisters saw the school burning and raced down the gravel road toward the oncoming fire truck, waving at the firemen as they turned into the school drive. By the time they got there, a couple of ranch boys who lived close by had arrived, and they cheered the firemen pouring water on the smoldering pile of gray ashes, cooling off the hot stone foundation. Must have been some hot embers from the wood stove that started the blaze, one of the firemen told the happy boys.

Bill's being late for chores—and a feeble excuse about some critter dragging off his trap and taking time to find it—led his mother to believe he'd been involved in the school fire. During supper that night, Wynona broached the schoolhouse fire and how it could have happened. The two girls giggled, kicking each other's feet, and then looked directly at Bill, who sat quietly looking down at his empty plate.

Bill's father said, "That's enough book learning for the boys anyway. They'll learn more by working full time on the ranch. The two young girls can go across the fields to Antelope Butte School on Prairie Road, and it won't be a whole lot further." Within a few days the subject of the schoolhouse burning vanished, and nothing ever came of it. Both boys acquired a workaholic obsession for the ranch, and all went smoothly until Tom's name topped the draft list. At that point the two girls had to pitch in and help do outdoor daily chores. Tom served in the European Theater in the Second World War and came back to work on the ranch full time. Within days after Tom arrived home, both girls lit out for town life. Several years later both parents passed away, and the boys inherited the homestead holdings. Neither Bill nor Tom ever married. From sunrise to sunset, they worked the ranch, raised a myriad of livestock and a big garden for table use, and never went to town except for canned groceries, work clothes, or implement parts. In dire need of better living quarters, Tom ordered a precut house, sight unseen, from the Montgomery Ward catalog, delivered as freight in two big trucks. Between chores they built the house from the ground up and, when the last interior walls got Sheetrocked, moved in. Soon after that, Tom died and Bill's enthusiasm waned for completing the interior altogether. For all the years I knew Bill, the hardwood floors were never completed; the jambs, castings and doors were never hung; and the inside walls were never taped or painted.

One day, over reheated black coffee and apple pie my wife had made for Bill, I mentioned to him that I like to hang doors and would be more than happy to help. He half smiled and said, "That sounds like a good winter project." Never did ask him again.

On what would be my last visit, Bill saw me coming, stopped the tractor, and raised the two-bottom plow. It glistened in the bright sun. As I drove up, he was already down off the tractor pulling clumps of golden prairie grass collected around the hitch-bar. Because he was being so fussy, I could tell he was waiting to tell me something. Turning toward me, he pointed down the creek.

"Hi, Ben," he said. "About a half hour ago, when I first broke ground, a nice big bunch of those little chickens flushed in front of the tractor. They went that way."

"Thanks for telling me. How've you been?" I ask.

"Good." he said, "I'll bet those dogs of yours can find them."

After talking for some time, Bill said quietly, "Better get back to my chores," and climbed slowly up into the yellow tractor seat.

After Bill died, the place sold and lost its character and charm. But locked in my mind, I still remember Bill's wonderful boyhood stories and visualize the richness of his place for wildlife.

BIRD DOGS
Bobbie Williams

We have always had from two to fourteen-plus pointing dogs. The "plus" stands for the many litters of puppies that added joy to our lives.

The emotion bond between Ben and his dogs is heartfelt. The affection he has for them is palpable.

Working on a project in his studio with several dogs roaming freely is truly Ben's Best Day Yet.